The Journal Keeper

The
Journal Keeper

A Memoir

PHYLLIS THEROUX

ATLANTIC MONTHLY PRESS
NEW YORK

Published simultaneously in Canada
Printed in the United States of America

FIRST EDITION

ISBN-13: 978-0-8021-1897-4

Atlantic Monthly Press
an imprint of Grove/Atlantic, Inc.
841 Broadway
New York, NY 10003

Distributed by Publishers Group West

www.groveatlantic.com

10 11 12 13   10 9 8 7 6 5 4 3 2 1

For R

Contents

The Journal Keeper

Introduction

In 1972, after our third and last child was born, we moved from a small frame house in Washington, D.C., into a gigantic frame house farther toward the edge of town. It was the house of my dreams, with seven bedrooms (the family moving out had raised eleven children there), a cozy kitchen, and a front window that looked out onto a 1950s-era neighborhood full of big trees and little children sucking popsicles as they whizzed down the street on their bicycles. As I stood in the front hall and mentally plugged in the Christmas tree, I knew I could spend the rest of my life here. What I didn't know was that "the rest of my life" was about to end.

Or did I? Looking back, there were signs, some of them quite large. But I wasn't interested in reading them. I wasn't interested in doing anything but working and reworking the classic Vogue pattern I had chosen for my life until it fit correctly. Step One: Get married. Step Two: Have children. Step Three: . . . This was the one that was giving me trouble.

A block away was a large park. On weekday mornings it was full of women like me, with downtown husbands who made our uptown lives possible. As they sat around the sandbox balancing their checkbooks or absentmindedly pushed toddlers on swings, I would search their smooth, pretty faces for clues. Were they happy, unhappy? Were they having trouble with Step Three, too? I couldn't tell. We were all so young that there were no lines on our faces to read between.

At night, after the children were asleep, I would sometimes slip out of the house and walk up to the park to be alone with my thoughts. In the dark, the houses on the perimeter of the playground looked like a stage set for Thornton Wilder's *Our Town*. Lying on the grass and looking up at the stars, I would listen to the muffled sounds coming through raised windows and match them up with scenes inside: someone playing with a dog, a joke-filled dinner party, a couple doing the dishes while they chatted about their children's report cards. The coziness of their lives filled me with longing.

In my own house, there were no scenes of any kind. Not even arguments. And the only sounds, apart from those of my children, were in my own head—or journal. Once, years later, I made the mistake of cracking one of them open. Out spilled the sighs and cries of my life as fresh as the day I had recorded them. I slammed it shut.

My earliest journals—a stenographer's notepad, a student composition book, an accountant's ledger—have a haphazard, impermanent look to them, as if I wasn't quite committed to the practice. I would grab whatever was nearest at hand to record my thoughts. Months go by without any entries. Often, I neglected to date them. The only consistent thread is my handwriting, taught by nuns with Esterbrook pens and calligraphy nibs. No matter how stormy the material, the words flow calmly and precisely across the page.

There were times when I poured my heart out. But other parts of my journals are quite different and dry-eyed. I note conversations overheard on airplanes, the way a beach looks at sunset, or—indecipherable to me now—I scribble down words—*authenticity, individuality, spectrum: old and new*—like clues in search of a unifying theory. A unifying theory of any kind was hard to find.

In the decade of the seventies, *Ms.* magazine was launched, Erica Jong wrote *Fear of Flying*, and the future for women, which for my generation looked like a well-maintained golf course when we graduated from college, was now anything we could make of it as long as we could find a babysitter. Down the street, one neighbor was holding ballet classes for children in her basement. Another woman had started a morning preschool. I began to write—both for myself and for publication. From the very beginning, my life and my writing were joined at the hip.

Shortly after we moved into the big house, I realized that it was not going to save me. One night, feeling restless, I got out of bed and went into a spare room off the porch where there was a desk and typewriter. Several hours later I got up and went back to bed. The next morning, I gathered up the pages that had fallen onto the floor and reread them. This is how it began:

Rocking slowly back and forth, pressing the worms in my chest against hunched-up knees. One little daughter banging for all she's worth against the front door. The baby, needing to be changed, crying in the backyard. A husband fixing the brakes on his bicycle on the patio. And I am rocking back and forth, not knowing where to place my hands, fix my gaze, or rest my soul.

This was a story about being caught in a life that I had been ill-advised on how to lead. Rolling the first page back into the typewriter, I gave it a title: "Getting the Hang of It." Perhaps

I could get it published, although my actual thoughts probably ran along the more commercial lines of *maybe this would sell.*

Manuscript in hand, I went down to the local drugstore and riffled through the magazine rack. My story was about a woman at home. Perhaps *Ladies Home Journal* matched it best. Writing the magazine's New York editorial address on a large manila envelope, I slipped the story inside and mailed it off without making a copy.

Our lives swing helplessly upon the smallest actions of other people. Six weeks later, an editorial assistant at *Ladies Home Journal* decided to have lunch at her desk and plucked my story from the slush pile of unsolicited manuscripts to read while she ate. A few days later, the phone rang. It was early evening and I was feeding my children supper.

"Mrs. Theroux, this is Dick Kaplan, managing editor of *Ladies Home Journal.*"

Our phone was in a small booth with a seat, off the kitchen. I sat down.

"We have your piece here, and I have two questions for you."

"Yes?"

"Well, first of all, are you all right?"

"Yes, I'm fine."

He seemed relieved, as if I might have been about to follow Sylvia Plath's head into the oven. "Oh, good. We were a little worried about you up here. We would like to publish your piece. We can offer you $500."

After the conversation was over, I sat in the phone booth and gazed back into the kitchen where my children were still scrabbling around with their fingers in plates of spaghetti. Perhaps, I thought, I had found something that wouldn't come undone. Perhaps there was something I knew how to do.

In fact, I didn't. I was writing beyond my ability. That small burst of competence, born out of a strong need to figure out what was happening to me, was a gift, a loan against a talent that had yet to be developed. The practice of writing, of laboring long hours to buckle words around an idea and make a sentence slide across the page like Fred Astaire across a dance floor, lay ahead of me. But when I hung up the phone, I was a different person with different possibilities. A five-page story without an ending had changed my life.

When people say something *changed their life,* I think they usually mean, upon deeper examination, that something has revived their imagination. A door we didn't know existed, or always thought was locked, suddenly swings open. Old ambitions, which we were too timid or thought we were too unqualified to realize, are gathered up and reconsidered. A talent judged too small is reevaluated.

Growing up, for example, I had wanted to be a child saint, which wasn't possible because I couldn't find a way to prove my sanctity. Moving on, I decided to be a saintly child movie star, but I couldn't find a talent scout to discover me. Finally, and more seriously, I hoped to be a devoted wife and mother whose husband (also devoted) would be a lifelong companion. We would look like the von Trapp family, without the dirndls, with lots of three-part harmony as we did the dishes.

Children are born with imaginations in mint condition, able to leap tall buildings in a single bound. Then life corrects for grandiosity. I was no exception. My early dreams did not materialize. But when I became a writer, I saw similarities between them all.

Being a writer does not have the global reach of a canonized saint but, at its best, writing is a deeply spiritual act that can have a profound effect upon the practitioner. Writing is not acting but, for someone who likes to entertain, it is a way of being onstage without worrying about camera angles. And while writing is not anything like being a mother of small children, I found most of my best writing material close at hand, which is where my children happened to be standing as well.

At the end of the day, after they were asleep, I would go upstairs to my desk, take out the file of fragments I was working on, and reread what I had written the night before. During the day, while I unscrewed peanut butter jars, sorted laundry, and worried about my marriage, it comforted me to think that no matter how much I slipped and fell on the ground floor of my life, that in the attic where I worked there was a slim sheaf of words that maintained their freshness and integrity whenever I returned to them.

Night after night, I would spin memories into paragraphs that didn't have a larger context: a stand of cockleweeds behind the summerhouse that blazed with dew in the early morning, a conversation with my grandmother, the way it felt to be alone on the playground when everybody else seemed so effortlessly popular. Later, many of these fragments would find a place in a memoir. But before I wrote for publication I simply wrote—like a woman in labor who wants to give birth to something inside that is ready to be born.

Five years later I was divorced, with three young, emotionally wounded children, living in the same house of my dreams that was suddenly too big and drafty to heat on a freelance writer's salary. But I was beginning to get assignments from magazines and newspapers. On the same day I signed a separation agreement, the first of a dozen essays I would write for the *New York Times* was published—which was thrilling, in a depressing kind of way.

While my personal life was going down in flames, my professional life was rising with the same speed from the ashes. But it seemed like a Faustian bargain that had been made without my consent: worldly success in exchange for personal ruin. It would be many years before I could view it in any other way.

My career began at a fortuitous moment. Women were feeling the ground shift dangerously beneath their feet. Magazines and newspapers were actively looking for new writers who could speak for them. I turned out essays, editorials, and feature pieces at a fast clip, finding my inspiration where I spent most of my time—in the kitchen, at my neighborhood cooperative garden, or in my own head as I waited on the front porch for my children to come home from school.

At the same time, I began to keep a daily journal. I thought of it primarily as a ship's log that enabled me to keep track of my thoughts and feelings as I bumped from one drama-filled day to the next. But I used it for other things as well: a place in which to work out ideas, store metaphors, and save odd bits of dialogue the way a composer might jot down small, incomplete bars of music. There were times, in the beginning, when I used my journal as a wailing wall, but I learned not to immortalize the darkness. Rereading it was counterproductive. What I needed was a place in which to collect the light.

Recently, it occurred to me that these journals might be a source of light for others as well. I had been struggling to write about my mother, who spent the last five years of her life with me. Two years before she died I began work; after her death, I intensified my efforts. But as time went on I got lost in the process, increasingly unsure how to make my mother come alive. Surrounding me were notes, letters, photographs, and journals—all the material I needed. Yet for such a quiet unworldly woman, she was proving more difficult to get down on paper than Eleanor Roosevelt.

Was my ego getting in the way? Was I overreaching? Or, as one astute writer friend of mine suggested, "Perhaps you need to set your mother aside for a while and work on something a bit easier—like editing your journals." The minute she said it, I grabbed at the lower bar.

What could be easier than editing one's own journals? I fell into the assignment the way one falls onto a bed full of pillows. This wasn't even writing; it was transcribing. Details that had been lost, like puzzle pieces in the sofa cushions, were retrieved and pressed back into the larger picture. Events that had come unglued from the calendar were put back in chronological order. But until I sat down to read all my journals in one fell swoop, I was largely unaware of one reality that soon struck me as deeper and more profound than anything I had written. As one year followed upon another, it became increasingly apparent to me that a hand much larger and more knowing than my own was guiding my life and pen across the page.

I am not referring here to automatic writing—although what writer would turn it down if it was good enough—or angels, although I have often had a sense of being gently pushed around by benevolent forces whose job it was to make sure I didn't take any wrong roads or miss any significant markers. It just never occurred to me to look in my journals for proof. But there, right before my eyes, were numerous examples of "managed care" where random events followed one another in a kind of planned, compassionate order, unimportant decisions turned out to be pivotal, and, in several instances, huge unrealistic wishes I had written down, primarily to get them off my chest, were granted.

"There is guidance for each of us," wrote Ralph Waldo Emerson, "and by lowly listening we shall hear the right word." *Lowly listening*—to my own inner voice—was what I had been doing almost every morning for the past thirty years, sitting quietly with my journal. The thoughts I recorded were like ballast in my hold. When I closed my journal to begin the day I felt properly weighted, not so easily blown off course. Only later did I grasp that keeping a journal not only saved my life in the record-keeping sense but saved it in a deeper, more mysterious sense as well.

When this book begins I am sixty-one and living with my eighty-two-year-old mother, who developed macular degeneration and had moved in with me three years earlier.

Absent from the pages are most references to my children, who have suffered enough beneath the point of my pen and deserve a little privacy. Missing, too, are most specific dates, which don't seem necessary. With the exception of the week of September 11, 2001, there are very few. But when I anticipate a question or think a particular entry could stand a little more explanation, I have added a few words. Otherwise, the journal simply unfolds alongside my life.

There are recurring themes: the struggle to write, self-doubt, my students and teaching life, living in a small town, loneliness, the care and repair of friendships, aging. Particularly aging. I am preoccupied with time and how often I abuse it. Financial worries come and go, as do I—to Italy and California, where I have conducted writing seminars that helped ease those worries. And weaving lightly through the pages is my mother, who came to live with me at a time in my life when we both qualified for senior citizen discounts at the movies. *The Journal Keeper* is ostensibly about my life, but I wound up painting a portrait of my mother in the margins, and perhaps this suits her best. Limelight always made her nervous.

Over the years I have read numerous journals, primarily by writers and artists whose thoughts inspire and jump-start my own: Marcus Aurelius, John Muir, Etty Hillesum, Anne Truitt. One can skip around the centuries the way one skips around a roomful of good friends who are always ready to drop everything for another heart-to-heart conversation. Sharing my journal with a third person, as I am doing here, simply expands the dialogue.

Whether it is possible to persuade someone else to keep a journal who isn't already doing it, I don't know. But one thing is certain. It doesn't depend on whether you have the time. When my children were young, I woke up before they did or waited until the end of the day when they were asleep, to *make* the time. Keeping a journal is like smoking (and for a while I did both together): if you need to do it, you will find a way. In fact, finding my way is why I took up journal-keeping in the first place. I was, to paraphrase Dante, in the middle of a dark wood. My journal was a flashlight. It still is.

In my midforties, I went through a very painful love affair. Toward the end, when the phone never rang and the silence was like a sharp knife carving out the interior walls of my heart, I was sitting quietly in my own despair when I heard a voice. It wasn't my voice. It wasn't anybody else's voice either. But it came from such a deep and delphic place within my being that I did not question its authority: *What is true cannot be taken from you. What is false will not remain.* I reached for a scrap of paper and wrote it down.

There have been very few times in my life when a voice this clear has spoken to me. Most mornings when I sit down with my journal, listening for a worthwhile thought to set down, I am the only source of the material. But every once in a while a deeper wisdom, trying to speak beneath the din, breaks through. Some days I am quiet enough to hear it. Other days, all I can hear is the soft scrape of my felt-tip pen as it makes its way across the page. But I have acquired the habit of listening—the way a servant listens for the sound of the bell—as if my life depended upon it.

Ashland, Virginia
2009

Living in a small town is like being in a play. I think of the people in Ashland as characters who wake up every morning in an ongoing story and position themselves onstage for another sixteen hours of walking, talking, and doing. Our scripts are mostly in our heads, although underlying the action is the question, "How will we make our mark upon the world today?" For the most part this is an illusion. It is the world that makes its mark upon us.

2000

In my experience you can have ability without leisure, but ability only, and not creativeness. Real ideas come to me while relaxed and brooding, meditative, passive. Then the unexpected happens. An illumination, a combination of words, a revelation for which I had made no conscious preparation.

—Bernard Berenson, *Sunset and Twilight*

A Monday morning

All the neighborhood children are back in school. I am surrounded by teachers, too—everything from a book I'm reading by art critic Bernard Berenson (who writes of lost leisure) to a new pair of secondhand lace curtains that redefine the light coming through my living room window.

The difference between knowledge and illumination is the difference between electric light and sun. It is not only the range but the quality of the light upon a subject. Sitting in the living room this morning, I needed my lamp before the sun rose above the tree line. But now the living room is radiant with natural light, every surface polished and picked out, and my lamp is unnecessary. I reach up and turn it off.

I am aware that these are the refined thoughts of a refined life, but I am also conscious of being deliberately apart from the homeless man holding up a sign for food on the Cary Street overpass as I stop for the light. He looks at me to see if I am looking at him to give him money. But I do not linger on his face, only brush over it. He sees a white woman in a white car, clean hands on a leather-wrapped steering wheel, sealed off by classical music playing on the radio. Who am I to say that holding up a sign asking for help isn't real work?

Today I spent almost a hundred dollars on books and music and am ashamed of the way I brushed past another beggar on the street, showing him empty hands as I made my way into a bookstore with Mozart and horn concertos on my mind. I needed them, I thought, to become deeper spiritually. Recently, I have "needed" a lot more: a new tape deck, air conditioning, a kitchen floor.

Last night I took Fitzgerald's *The Great Gatsby* off the shelf to reconnect with great writing. The amazing phrases that seem so simply made, like *burning gardens,* were there to remind me of what is possible. I have reread a lot of my own earlier writing, and I seem to be writing more simply now. That being said, I do not have the easy access to the fires of creativity I once had.

This morning I took a walk around the streets of Ashland and collected trash. This is great training for the eye and mind. Dislodging a plastic bag from a bramble or emptying a beer can full of mud before putting it in my sack is like cleaning up an essay. The better it looks, the more motivated I am to continue the process.

My house is like an essay. As I sit here in this wing chair, I notice the pillow that lies at the wrong angle, a lamp that should be a little closer to the edge of the table, a curtain not quite in alignment with the window frame. I am restless until I have made the adjustments, moved, turned, or pulled everything to where, from where I sit, they ought to be.

Opening Gary Zukav's *The Seat of the Soul* this morning, my eye fell upon these lines:

As you face your deepest struggles, you reach for your highest goal. . . . This is the work of evolution. It is the work that you were born to do.

In Charlottesville, Virginia, for the Virginia Festival of the Book, where I took part in an authors' reading

I am sitting in the Omni Hotel, a few tables away from Reynolds Price, who is in his wheelchair, eating breakfast with a companion. He gazes my way as I am spooning some yogurt into my mouth, and I wonder if he is mentally putting words to the sight of a woman eating yogurt, as I am doing the equivalent to him.

Price spoke last night to a large crowd. "A writer tends to be hard-wired for language," he said, recalling a boyhood spent sopping up the color and cadence of his family's way of talking. He recounted the story of his aunt, who had run out of money and was being consoled by her sister. "They can't get blood from a turnip," she was told. "No, but they can put the turnip in jail," she replied.

In another part of his talk, he said, "We come down to a personal reality. . . . We're born as people who love life or people who don't. . . . You can die pretty fast if you put your mind to it."

My thoughts are interrupted by a waiter who finds out I'm a writer and wants to know how it works. "What's involved?" he asks. "Do you write it yourself or get somebody to write it for you?" He tells me he has a friend, a golfing buddy, who wants to write a book, he's not sure about what. As for himself, he's not a reader except for the newspapers, but that's not very satisfying. "Everything's in the same style." Recently he bought a book on sale at the local bookstore.

"It's called *Nausea*. I got it for a dollar."

"By Sartre?"

"Yes. You know it?"

"He's pretty profound."

"That's what I like. I want to feel like I'm getting something out of it."

During the afternoon, I had a cup of coffee with a young friend who worries about how to keep her marriage strong, saying that whenever she hears about a friend getting engaged she thinks, *Oh, no*—"even though we're all right."

I reminisced about my own failed marriage and conceded that getting married again wasn't on my agenda. Uppermost on my mind was how to be fruitful. "I'm sixty-one," I told her, "and wondering how many more buds there are on the branch."

This morning I encountered this theme in a poem by George Herbert:

> *And now in age I bud again,*
> *After so many deaths I live and write;*
> *I once more smell the dew and rain,*
> *And relish versing. . . .*

What I realized from being with all those writers in Charlottesville was that I was with people who use their imaginations as easily and unself-consciously as other people use a towel. That was the thrill: to go to different authors' readings and listen as men became women and women became men and writers got inside the hundred-year-old heads of Alamo survivors. This is no different from acting, and I wonder if I can take some new steps on a new stage. In many ways, I have taken no risks and made no changes for a long time, if ever. This is no way to live.

The life of most writers without an independent income is full of risk and re-invention. I have supported myself, some years much better than others, in the usual way: writing books, magazine articles, and newspaper columns; teaching; editing; and working on a series of oral histories. Once, particularly short of funds, I took on a woman whose big dream was to have a story accepted for the Little Golden Books series. She came to my house with a double-spaced manuscript about Tommy Turtle running away from home. I felt I'd sunk pretty low when I heard myself say, "Well, if you had Tommy Turtle get into a scrap with Bucky Beaver before he joins up with Dilly Duck, it might make the plot more interesting." But when I wrote the journal entry about the

Charlottesville festival, I wasn't thinking about money but about how I had always stayed within a certain genre of writing, one in which I already knew I could excel: the personal essay. Perhaps it was possible to move in another direction. This was the first time I had seriously posed the question to myself on paper. Posing the question was the first step.

Last night I went to Duncan Memorial Church to hear Pastor John Kinney preach. It was riveting, hilarious, challenging, and showy. The part that moved me most was the story he told about himself when he was a little boy and thought he was lost, only to feel his father's hand fall upon his shoulder. "'I was lost!' said the boy. 'No, you weren't,' said his father. 'I had my eye on you the whole time. I knew where you were.'" Tears sprang to my eyes. Maybe the truth is that I feel lost more often than I want to admit.

Sitting in a church full of white people listening to a black preacher, I was full of judgment. When it came time to sing a gospel hymn, several of the white women in the choir couldn't clap in time. Their hands were like dead fish, flapping any old way to the music. It made me scornful. Not to be able to clap was pathetic. But then I realized that the urge to find fault was rooted in my own insecurity. I tried to see them with more loving eyes and realized that these were women wanting to be part of the music, trying to get it together. They had terrible timing but their faces were lit up, delighted to be part of something that had some life.

There is something very wrong with my use of time. To walk into the house after being away twenty-four hours and immediately get pulled into the mail on the table, messages on my phone, and e-mail on my computer, while barely having time to say hello to Mother, who has been waiting all day for me to return, is out of kilter. I cannot be in real time without wondering what other people have done or said in virtual time. Before voice mail and the Internet, there was a decent interval between cause and effect; one was forced to wait patiently on the other side of the door until someone opened it. But now, with time and distance being reduced to a nanosecond, my ability to delay gratification is weakened.

This morning, clearing away bamboo from the back part of the garden, I mused over the way you have to reverse the processes of mind and body as you get older. It is natural when young to want to be physically on the move all the time. The struggle is to sit still long enough to get the mind's attention. When you get older, the process is reversed. The body must be kicked into motion against a growing inclination to rest awhile longer while the mind continues to move at breakneck speed.

I sometimes pretend to be someone else of superior abilities in order to get something done. While cleaning my room, for example, I pretend to be my neighbor Mary Lou Brown, who is extremely meticulous and organized. It is a way of manipulating reality, of tricking myself into a higher level of performance. On the tennis court, I'll sometimes pretend to be a recently recovered polio victim, which makes every stroke miraculous.

But when I'm not pretending, I know there is a strictness about life that lurks just beneath the surface. When we do not obey life's laws—in everything from love to digestion—that strictness surfaces. For months my stomach has bothered me with heartburn (what does it say about the developed world that the most popular over-the-counter pills are for heartburn and acid indigestion?), but until now I would not give up coffee. Today, having done so for less than a night, my stomach has responded with restored health.

This morning my thoughts center upon what I perceive to be the rough justice of God working within each one of us. We are driven to deliver the truth inside us, no matter what we do to avoid or bury it. How to deliver it is the challenge. It is not just about using our reason although, like a diving board, we must use it to its limit, running to its very end. But then we must leap—like a spark—into the air. It is that spark that illuminates the understanding, makes the heat and the difference.

Last night, meditating on the sentence *Be still, and know that I am God,* I thought that if I was still, truly still, for even a moment, I could probably step through the wall that divides the human from the divine consciousness.

In April, I held a writing seminar at an inn on the north-coast town of Mendocino, California. The drive through the Anderson Valley to the ocean never fails to cleanse my eye.

To get to Mendocino, you take 101 to Cloverdale and cut across the Anderson Valley, which is like driving through Steinbeck's "pastures of heaven": with bright green hills tender with new grass, sheep, and ribbons of water flowing down the banks that head toward the Navarro River. Then, finally, out to the open sea and our inn, full of cut flowers and decanters of sherry. Sitting on the inn's porch, framed by two posts, I see the essence of Mendocino between them: pines on one side, eucalyptus trees on the other, and, floating like ivory trumpets in the meadow, the wild calla lilies, mixed with brambles and blackberry bushes that tumble down the cliff to the sea. In the background one hears the scrubbing noise of surf, a distant grinding of lumber trucks rounding the curve, cowbells clanging. I rejoice, I rejoice.

After the seminar, I drive south to San Rafael to visit the Dominican convent campus where I went to high school. Whole rooms of the past open up as I drive down Grand Avenue. My nose remembers more than my eyes. The sharp oily smell of eucalyptus combines with afternoon dust from the hockey field in Forest Meadows. But my heart feels the difference between then and now. Where is my former French instructor, who was just married when she came to teach? My Latin teacher, Sister Gregory, is now senile in the convent infirmary. We are all slowly moving off the stage.

At the new campus in San Anselmo, where I am a guest of the school for one night, I peek into classrooms that are full of little children, soft as the hills in springtime, with new skin, hair, and questions. I wish my grandchildren could go to school here.

At mass in the school chapel this morning, a priest spoke about feeling lost, which again brought tears to my eyes.

In the gospel, Jesus is chiding his disciples who want him to show them the Father. He says, "After all this time, you do not know that to be with me is to be with the Father?" One of the women in the chapel asked for prayers for a forgotten playmate of mine who used to live near me in San Francisco. She was a pale, pretty girl with large eyes, who grew up to have four children and four husbands, plus several bouts with cancer.

After dinner I walked back to the campus room where I was spending the night. The fog had rolled over the top of the mountain and hung, like a thick white quilt, halfway down the side. If I ever live here I will never get used to that kind of beauty.

Mother's view of most people's lives is that they are caught in an eternal round of rituals that keep them from facing the truth or experiencing life at first hand. We are pulled along by an endless progression of holidays, showers, birthdays, funerals, and special prepackaged days like Mother's Day, from one year to the next. "They can't get separate from"—she crooks her two index fingers in the shape of a set of quotation marks—"the tribe."

I woke this morning with two words in my head, "Go deeper." Reading aloud to Mother from George Crane's book *Bones of the Master,* helps me know how. Crane is like me, too tied to words, too dependent upon thought. "Here I am," he writes, as he follows behind the old monk, Tsung Tsai, in a walking meditation, "fooling myself with the search for words that would explain everything."

He says to Tsung Tsai, "The world is so difficult to give up."

Tsung Tsai nods. "Attachment very strong. Don't worry. When you go away, just come back."

Attachment is so easily confused in my mind with love, which gives attachment legitimacy. Yet I can see the difference in other, more developed persons, who project a kind of compassionate awareness and appreciation of those they love but don't leave fingerprints all over them.

A few days ago, at Cross Brothers Market, I was at the checkout counter when an elderly large-bellied white man in overalls and suspenders, a farmer type, came into the store with a five-year-old child who looked as if she was the product of black and white parents. She had golden skin and kinky brown hair. They seemed easy with each other, the way grandchildren and grandparents should be, and as they rounded the corner I heard him say to her softly, "Now, let's see about that ice cream." One should always expect the unexpected.

Living in a small town is like being in a play. I think of the people in Ashland as characters who wake up every morning in an ongoing story and position themselves onstage for another sixteen hours of walking, talking, and doing. Our scripts are mostly in our heads, although underlying the action is the question, "How will we make our mark upon the world today?" For the most part this is an illusion. It is the world that makes its mark upon us.

Tonight, walking through the dark streets after visiting with Susan and Woody Tucker (Woody's mother had just died), I was aware of being a small strand in the fabric that makes the town hold together better. It is not exciting work but it is something to be grateful for—knowing that sitting with someone at their kitchen table, talking about their mother, makes a difference,

Yesterday I tried to do one thing, begin an essay "On Single-mindedness." I created a page of notes and then the phone rang. It was my younger son, telling me that he had just run into his old childhood friend Max on a street corner in New York. Their first reaction was to think how happy their mothers would be that they were together. The second phone call was from Max's mother. There went the day.

The power of *Bones of the Master* grows within me. "Don't think," Tsung Tsai tells Crane. "Thinking weakens." I am becoming aware of this truth. Thinking can tyrannize, introduce willfulness and fear.

I feel at the age of sixty-one that I should be a sage, not a novice. It is embarrassing to be so shallow. Yet it is also important to be aware of how raw and unlettered I really am and to be eager to learn something new.

This morning I awoke determined to reinvigorate my life by disciplining myself so that the Goddess of Comfort is put in her proper place. Up at seven, make the bed, prune my life so that the strength flows into fewer branches.

Yesterday Mother turned eighty-three. Knowing how nervous she is about her birthday—the result of a childhood wound when her parents forgot to celebrate it one year—I said, "Let's just let the day unfold." She loved that. "Yes!" she exclaimed. "Wouldn't it be nice to have a birthday where people dropped in, not even knowing it was my birthday," "Sort of like a drive-by birthday," I suggested. "That's right," she said.

The day proceeded like the slow unwrapping of a gift. In the morning, our next-door neighbor, Mel Titus, came over with her two boys and sat on the porch for several hours, drinking tea and telling us about her past. It was a quiet, happy start. Then, after lunch, Katherine Tinker arrived with a present of some superior scotch and stayed to talk about her husband, who has been diagnosed with multiple sclerosis. I told her my belief that most of us learn what we have to learn before we finish our lives. "Do you think so?" she asked. "I'm not so sure."

I decided to go upstairs and finish up Mother's birthday quilt on the sewing machine. Midafternoon, my cousin Angel drove down from Maryland as a surprise. I began cooking the birthday dinner around four. Guests began to arrive around six-thirty. They brought food, jars of flowers, and their talents: a song sung by the Reihl family, accompanied by their father on the guitar. After dinner, twelve-year-old Cody Artiglia brought out his collection of artifacts from Arizona, where his family had vacationed that June. They included owl throw-up and dinosaur poop. The day ended with sparklers and Roman candles on the lawn. We sat in a fairy circle of logs on the grass and watched little boys twirling sparklers in the warm sulfur-scented air.

Lately, I have been falling into the ways of my mother, sitting long and happily on the back porch, doing nothing except acting as if I, too, were eighty-three. We are now so well attuned to each other that our tastes and impulses are uncannily alike. I will think about what I'd like to cook for dinner only to be interrupted by my mother, who says, "I think I'll just have a baked potato," mirroring my own thoughts.

This morning, very early, I took a canoe ride on the nearby South Anna River with my neighbor, Ned Dillon, who has lived here all his life. The air was scented with mud and honeysuckle. As we eased down the river, we saw beaver slides, tangles of tree roots like piles of rope, and bright islands of river grass that we paddled around into deeper water. Ned is as easy as the South Anna to be with. He has known everyone in Ashland since childhood. The conversation turned to one of his childhood friends in town who reminds me of a character in an F. Scott Fitzgerald novel—tall, patrician, and slightly removed from most other people. Ned knew what I meant. "He got that way when he went to college," he said.

This is the height and heat of summer. Everything pants for water—dogs, hydrangeas, boys wanting to dive into a lake and feel the cold second skin coat their dusty bodies. Each day dissolves like a lozenge upon the tongue. I can barely recall it except to describe the flavor, and even that is ephemeral: phone calls, glasses of ice tea.

❧

Today I came downstairs at five-thirty and lit a stick of incense and a candle to focus the nose and eye. But my attention continually drifted. Finally, I turned on the light, took up my journal, and began to write, to give my mind a line of print to follow. It is discouraging to think of all these years that I have driven my mind to skin and bones, like an exhausted but dutiful horse, and now, when I try to dismount and tether it, it won't stop moving.

Why isn't it enough simply to enjoy a thing without wanting to describe it, pull the thread of sensibility through it, like a needle poking through a bead, to make it mine?

Looking back over the entries of the past few months, I see the idea of attention, pure attention, emerging in different forms and guises. Slowing down long enough to pay full attention requires an empty mind. We must clear the decks and be doing nothing else. This is what goes counter to the culture, which tries to distract and divide our attention so that it never rests on any one thing for any length of time.

A final thought: there are so many souls who could help me if only I remembered to invoke their help. Jesus; Baba Whatsisname; my old high school principal and mentor, Sister Maurice; the entire community of saints. They are all there and I believe available. Add to them the saints still on earth, Tsung Tsai, for example, and I am surrounded by my superiors.

Yesterday I entered a new phase, hopefully with grace. I was asked by my friend Mel if I could babysit eight-year-old Jesse while she went to a school meeting. A part of me resisted the offer. It implied that I was too old to have anything else to do. I could sense a little hesitation on Mel's part, as if she worried I would take her request amiss. But after thinking it over for a few moments I decided to be thrilled—and that made all the difference. And I did indeed have a great time, making Jesse popcorn, looking at the iguana in his aquarium, and reading him stories from his book of samurai tales. (He kept correcting my pronunciation until I said *samurai* the right way.)

In 1988, after living in Washington, D.C., for twenty-four years, I left town—reluctantly. Washington was where I had come as a new bride, had raised my children, created a much-loved community of friends, established myself as a writer, and gone through a divorce—more or less in that order. My roots were deep, but the desire to own my own home (which I had to sell in 1984) was deeper. Between 1984–88, I rented, while real estate prices continued to climb higher and higher. Sick of throwing monthly rent checks over my shoulder, I began to think about moving. North was more expensive than south.

One day, a realtor friend told me about a house for sale outside of Richmond, Virginia. The next weekend, I drove down to take a look. Ashland was a sleepy little town with big trees and no stoplights. I remember seeing a John Deere tractor dealership and an advertisement for a Jell-O wrestling contest on the main *street. Ahead of me, as I bumped across the railroad tracks, was a pickup truck with a Confederate flag on its back window. Turning down a shady side street, I pulled up in front of a two-story brick house with no landscaping. It looked solid but unloved. There were bookshelves and a fireplace in the living room, the closet doors opened without falling off their hinges, and the light was good. I could live here, I thought. Some of the biggest decisions take the least amount of time. Thirty minutes later, I made an offer. Over the years, I found professional and personal reasons to return to Washington frequently. But every time I did, I bumped into the same truth: I had closed a chapter in my life and could not easily add on new pages.*

You have to stay in your old neighborhood in order to maintain the right to drop in on people. Here in Washington I realized there weren't that many people I could—or wanted to—see. Judy O'Hara wasn't home, Donna and Rita are both gone (dead), and Faith is too nervous to drop in on unannounced. I went to the nearby Starbucks, which used to be the dry cleaners. At 8:30 A.M. it was full of strapping well-dressed men with soft hair and hard bodies. They ordered their skim decaf cappuccinos and exuded intelligence and worldliness. I wanted to know them all, be part of all their worlds—an impossibility that throws me back upon the truth that the only person I have the absolute right (and obligation) to know is myself.

Later, I visited my old cooperative garden in Rock Creek Park, which has become a citadel of netted enclosures. "It's the deer," explained one gardener, a bright-eyed woman in her early fifties who is a nurse at NIH. She was married to two different Frenchmen, living in France for twenty years before divorcing the last one and coming home "to get some benefits. My life is nowhere near as dramatic as it was, but I've

29

made a good life for myself here. It's simple, except when I complicate it." From a bag she took some cotton seeds she was planning to plant and showed them to me. "I'm going to grow my own underwear," she joked.

I wonder whether one day my children will feel the same pull backward that I am feeling now. Does there come a time in most people's lives when the urge to explore gives way to the lure to return to the first places in our lives? And is this a temptation or a legitimate impulse?

The bench I'm sitting on is, I'm told, a memorial to a child who died. There is no plaque but it is a sturdy, comfortable bench, just right for sitting and thinking about the perishability of life. Mr. Olson, the garden's overseer, is gone, except in the memory of a few other gardeners. Mr. Khoury, who used to come here with his wife toward the end of his life, is gone, too.

The garden was the highlight of my visit to Washington. Twenty years ago, struggling with wounded children, a perilous financial picture, and men who didn't fit the bill, I recouped a sense of peace and good fortune when I was digging in my ten-by-twenty-foot plot here. To be surrounded by towering trees in a city felt luxurious and lucky. Standing in the garden, surrounded by sunflowers, dahlias, cucumbers, and squash plants, softened me, filled me with a sense of plenty. That feeling has not changed.

When my children were young, I supplemented my income with writing seminars (called Nightwriters) around my dining room

table. Later, I taught in a back room in the nearby Politics & Prose bookstore. And eventually, when my children had flown the coop, I flew, too—teaching wherever I found the right combination of shabby-chic accommodations, delicious food, and a beautiful location. In July of 2000, I conducted my first (and so far only) Nightwriters seminar in Scotland, on the Isle of Mull.

I have just returned from three weeks on the Isle of Mull. The exhaustion I feel is from having to be so alert and so unproductive at the same time. When one is in receiver mode, always absorbing something new or beautiful, trying to understand or fit in, it is not possible to be in a transmitting mode as well. But to live for three weeks on an island where the sea, the sky, and the mountains are in front of you at all times clears the imagination like a windshield that has been wiped free of grime. I am not alone in this feeling. People remark upon the distilled quality of the light on Mull, how their eyes seem to sharpen and improve the longer they are there.

It is the smallness and inaccessibility of Mull that gives the island life its grace and necessary slowness. Single-lane roads force a courtesy upon drivers, who must pull over to let an oncoming driver pass. The water creates a barrier between ourselves and instant gratification. You want film developed? It must go by ferry to Oban on the mainland and come back again a week later. There is no cable for television reception. Instead, you look out the window for entertainment.

Yesterday, while waiting in my friend Magi's hospital suite for her neck operation to be over, I read through Jacques Lusseyran's *And There Was Light*. There was much to think about.

Lusseyran was totally blind, but able to "see" in a way that enabled him to be an invaluable member of the French Youth Resistance. (His capacity to "read" a prospective new member's voice, to know whether he or she was genuine or a spy, was near-perfect.) Then, when he was fifteen he temporarily lost his capacity to perceive what he could not see. But a voice inside told him that, "I had fallen into a trap, had forgotten the true world: the world within, which is the source of all the others. I must remember that this world, instead of disappearing, would grow with the years, but only on one condition: that I believe in it unshakably."

Yesterday, playing tennis, I realized that many of my problems stem from not remaining in my body, but rather "leaking" into the past or future. Being on a tennis court in Ashland reminds me of being on a tennis court in California, so my imagination carries me there, which makes it hard for me to connect with the ball in Virginia. But if I consciously pull myself back to the center of my self, I create a field of gravity and my powers are somewhat restored.

My friend Magi talks about her work as a professional mediator and how one must be 100 percent present and listening. She said this would be a good exercise for me, that sometimes I am not present or if I am she's always conscious that I may leave in an instant. Other people have told me the same thing, that sometimes I take little out-of-body trips while they're talking to me. Not good.

I miss my children, each for reasons the other two cannot supply, which is as it should be. This stage of parenthood is impossible to imagine until you're in it.

When I think about why people have children, I realize how little it should have to do with the future. If, before any children are conceived, we knew that our reward for raising them would be perhaps several phone calls a month, a very occasional visit, and the sense of having once been important in their lives, we might not do it. But if we realize that the rewards are given during the raising, we will calculate the cost differently. My children have taught me more than I have taught them, given me more joy than I have given them, and their not being present or even much aware of me now does not alter this.

∾

IN NEW YORK CITY

I met George Crane, author of *Bones of the Master,* today. He was easy to talk to, a real writer. "I don't know what I would do," he said, "if I wasn't writing poetry." He works a full writer's day, about four hours, and moves houses often. He has only lived in Accord (New York) for about a year. He has warm brown eyes and masses of silver hair. We talked a lot about Tsung Tsai, how he is an authentic mystic. George has seen him perform some amazing feats. It was good to be with him. Things I rarely confess about what I truly feel about myself, such as my fear of being hard-hearted, came pouring out.

Waiting in Penn Station for the train back to Virginia, I watched a young girl, perhaps seventeen or eighteen, who was also waiting. There was an expectant, self-contained happiness about her that had everything to do with what she was thinking about—perhaps a boyfriend who was going to meet her at the other end. Her thoughts competed with her eyes, which gazed out at the flow of travelers, but she was only mildly, idly interested, following someone for just a few yards before returning to the more brightly lit interior of her own mind. She was so fresh and innocent, like a soap scrubbed schoolgirl, clutching her plum-colored garment bag, which matched her plum-colored luggage.

Mentally, I took a ball of string and wound it around everybody there, from the little boy playing cards on his suitcase, to the couple kissing in the corner, to the rabbi leaning against the wall reading. By the end I had created a cat's cradle of connections between everybody in Penn Station. When one person moved, everybody else moved, too, in a kind of string dance. I think, on another level, that is really what happens. We influence each other, but so subtly that we cannot trace it back.

Now back in Ashland, I am exactly where I would want to be if I weren't already here. Last night, reading Wendell Berry's poems, I could feel an old theme—the inseparability and connectedness of everything—reemerge. Everything— from the books to the sofa to the game of Chinese checkers on the table—is intimately related, like my past, which echoes in my head as I walk down old streets and remember being young with a mop of curly hair, in a blue coat, searching through the racks for my future and a dress to wear in it.

Reading a great poet acts like a rope that pulls me out of the weed-choked creek into the broader river. Suddenly I feel cold water around me. I am in the depths again.

❧

This morning the porch door was locked, meaning that Mother had not risen during the night. I always wonder, when these small routines aren't followed, whether she has died. But when I walked into the room she was only sleeping.

Last night, aware that Mom's eyes were depriving her of too much joy, I went into her room and told her I knew this. She conceded that it wasn't easy and asked if I would read her one of the scraps of paper that she keeps in a wallet by her bed. I pulled one out. On it she had written, "What your intentions are create your reality." We talked about that for a while. It is not so easily understood as it sounds.

❧

Reading Alice Miller's *Drama of the Gifted Child* is difficult. There is a strident, insistent quality to it. But her question is valid: Why is it that otherwise bright and sensitive children are emotionally blank about important things, like the birth of a rival younger sibling? I don't remember my younger brother John's birth but I was angry at him—for reasons that remain beyond my comprehension—for my entire childhood.

❧

Home, after a third trip to Italy and a Nightwriters seminar. It was a rich time with a rewarding group of writers, although not without "moments." Women are complicated and—when we get what we need, primarily love and confirmation—fantastically supportive. But when we don't get it, sparks fly. I had to confront one student who was being difficult, and I began by saying something I wasn't sure was true—that I loved her. Instantly, when I heard my own words, I realized it was true. By drawing a finger in the sand, I had created both the channel and the love that flowed down it. You attract the love you describe.

Mother's first words as I walked in the door were about the leaves falling. "It's all about detachment," she said. "I can actually hear it when I sit on the porch and listen to them fall."

Later, sitting in Dorothy Jones's kitchen, I was aware of how the air in her house has the thick flavor of dust, sunlight, old books, fried chicken, and furniture polish. It is a human, comforting smell. Clutter is a part of it. A sense of belonging is another. It is such a gift to coincide with where you live. Ashland has become that place for me.

Yesterday's gifts: a Stanley Kunitz poem ("The Layers"), a brilliant day, and my mother's continuing presence and example. She is so gentle, without the need to proselytize. I see myself as insistent and demanding, pushing my opinions on others. It would be better if I didn't have any opinions at all, since it's so difficult for me to hold them quietly.

Some of the child's clear eye is clouded over by ideas and opinions, preconceptions and abstractions. . . . Not until years later does an instinct come that a vital sense of mystery has been withdrawn. The sun glints through the pines, and the heart is pierced in a moment of beauty and strange pain, like a memory of paradise. After that day . . . we become seekers. —Peter Matthiessen

Sometimes the only way I can write, when I have nothing to say myself, is to copy something significant from another writer.

As of this moment I am bill-free and paid up. It is, however, the beginning of a new month of bills to come. Without the income from a monthly column (my contract with *House Beautiful* magazine has just ended), I am vulnerable. Well, so be it. I must make an act of faith and go ahead with the new asphalt driveway.

This may be as good a place as any to say a few words about my attitude toward money, a topic that surfaces frequently in my journal, usually when I'm about to run out of it. As a freelance writer it helps to be independently wealthy, married to someone who has a regular job, or—failing that—have a regular job yourself. None of this has ever been true of me, at least for very long, and when I was getting divorced my lawyer kept asking me about assets I surely must have forgotten when I was making up the list. "No," I said, gesturing to my blue-jean skirt and thrift-shop sweater, "what you see is what you get." My lawyer, who was sitting beneath a plaque that read ASSUME NOTHING, smiled. "In my experience, women who look like you are often worth millions." But the facts are that while I have lived around wealthy people all my life, my own family consistently bought high and sold low until we had nothing but a bunch of scuffed-up antiques and some scrapbooks full of photographs of houses that were no longer ours.

On the subject of money, here's what I have going against me: an inability to sustain my interest in it for very long, a deep-seated belief that there is nothing I can do to better my economic position, and a relationship with my bank account that is akin to the relationship I have with my refrigerator. I rarely know what is in either one.

Here is what I have going for me: a belief that if I am doing my part to use my talents and lead a meaningful life the universe will play ball with me, and if it doesn't it's not my fault; a mother who once said, "If you take a step toward life, life will support you," which I have found to be true; and the ability to take a piece of chalk and draw a smaller circle around my feet when the old larger circle falls apart. I trace this last back to a sentimental childhood book The Five Little Peppers and How They Grew. The Pepper family was poor but merry, and if the lights got turned out they rejoiced in finding a candle to hold while they stood around the piano and sang songs in the dark.

More than once I have awoken from a fitful night with my hand clutching the windowsill above my bed. But this is simply my subconscious asserting its right to be heard, at least when I'm asleep. Awake, I have what my friend Ellen Papoulakos says is a teenager's view of money, that is, there is bound to be more on the way from somewhere. And I have something else: a keen awareness of death, which tends to put everything short of death in perspective.

An example: once I was sitting in my kitchen reading the newspaper. Suddenly, all three of the wooden shelves I had recently installed to hold my china and glassware crashed to the floor by my chair. (Screwing in brackets is not one of my strong points.) What did I do? I gazed down at the shards of crockery and glass on the floor—and turned to the editorial page.

Normally, I am not aware of the important role I play in my mother's life, but yesterday when she told me of her anxiety attack, which came upon her suddenly, I realized it. Before she went to sleep I gave her a back rub, massaged her face, and tucked the blankets around her ("It makes me feel safe," she said) before she went to sleep.

Thinking about Mother, I compare her to the late stage of a dandelion. All the earlier, fleshy brilliance is gone. Now she is a fluffy globe of light, holding herself erect as ever but ready, with one puff, to fly away, be gone.

Most of what goes through my head I don't record. It would be impossible. But some things want to become words, like the maple leaves in the jug on the kitchen windowsill. Every time I go to the sink they fill up my eye. In countless little moments I think of death, of its approach, not just to me but the yellow pepper on the sill, smooth as wax a week ago, now beginning to wrinkle.

Suppose I had nothing external with which to define myself. Take away my children, even my ex-husband, then remove my friends and family, then my books—those small but solid tokens of creativity and achievement, the basis of a reputation. Upon what, with whom, would I base my worth? How would I keep from feeling lost or meaningless? The answer, I know, lies within myself, the being or person who waits—passively or actively—at the center.

In the greater quiet of my life, I am able to listen to myself more easily. It is a new sensation, or realization, to know that I have what I call a Resident Adviser. Only now, after so many years, do I realize how incomplete, how painfully absent from myself I was when I was getting divorced, falling in and out of love, living in so much daily pain and longing.

∿

This morning, lying in bed, I felt surrounded by an enemy I could not vanquish. Depression fell. Then a thought. Be unattached from your feelings. Welcome them and try to learn what they have to impart.

∿

A TRIP TO CHARLOTTESVILLE WITH MY FRIEND BILL MCPHERSON

We walked around the University of Virginia quad designed by Jefferson. It is winter now, stacks of wood lie by each student's door. The ivy on the serpentine brick walls is withering, the gardens, laid out in pie-shaped triangles, are bare. Something in me doesn't like to take the time to describe what I'm looking at: the slender student bent over her book in Starbucks, the little snow-suited baby waiting patiently to be scooped up by its mother in the restaurant, the bundled-up Tibetans downtown sitting before their tables of trinkets and prayer flags. But another part of me wants to develop a more physically observing eye. This sabbatical from writing has given me the space and time to cultivate my eye for its own sake.

Increasingly, I am coming to view the brain as a large, unevenly frozen pond. Some sections—like the part that holds

childhood memories—are smooth and hard, with every mark of
the ice skate clearly delineated. Other, more recent, sections are
so crisscrossed and layered with impressions that no single mark
is visible. Then there are the parts that are too mushy to hold
anything at all. When you skate upon them, you fall through.

❧

There is something mysterious but obvious about the importance of staying put. The soul cannot do its work when we are
in constant motion. It requires the knowledge that it won't be
asked to move too far from home. These past several weeks
when I have been at rest within myself have been fruitful by
being fallow. I can feel my imagination repairing itself, my
powers of concentration returning.

Still, at some unacknowledged level, I have lost faith.
The passionate side of me has been submerged or doused, like
a fire gone out. Yet I resist thinking this, wondering whether
it is simply age. No, it is something else, more self-induced.

❧

Reading from Jacques Lusseyran's book *And There Was Light,* I
find this on page 11:

*As a young child I was not aware that I did not see well. I was not
concerned about it, because I was happy to make friends with light as
though it were the essence of the whole world.*

*Colors, shapes, even objects, the heaviest of them, all had the same
vibration. And today, every time I assume the attitude of tender attention, I find the same vibration once again.*

It is the phrase *tender attention* that moves my imagination. What I continually fail to note in these pages, is the heartbreaking, light-filled brilliance of the world I swim through like an unappreciative fish every day. Let the record show that I am grateful.

While still living in Washington, I started a story about a town that was halted in its tracks by a blizzard just before Christmas. It had a solid premise but after a few pages it lost its way, sounding like Betty MacDonald or Jean Kerr on a bad day. I had no experience writing fiction, but I liked the fragment well enough to take it with me when I moved to Ashland. Every so often I would get the story out of the drawer and try—without luck—to breathe life into it again. Then, just before this next entry, I imagined myself standing before the judgment seat of God and being asked, "Tell me, whatever happened to that idea I gave you back in 1986?" The fact that my mother would ask plaintively every so often if I was ever going to finish the story (read: "before I die") was an added incentive. I did a quick calculation of my time, which was ample, and money, which would run out in about three months, and decided that I didn't want to die without having given the story my best shot. "All right," I said, "I'll do it. But if it's not any good don't blame me." To which God replied, in Milton's voice, "Doth God exact day labor, light denied?" Actually, that's not what God said, but if this were a work of fiction. . . .

I have set out before me a number of projects that I would like to work on: my Christmas story, a book about my mother, a history of the Dominican sisters, and—on another track—a nonprofit wing of Nightwriters that would be devoted to bringing black and white teachers together to focus on the racism that divides us.

In my mind, this is the last day of the vacation that began when I returned from Italy. Tomorrow I return to my vocation, to myself. I know I will be tempted to fly in different directions—sending presents, making Christmas cards, folding laundry. Help me, God, to stare them down.

Yesterday went well. I worked on the plot outline for the Christmas book. No real writing, but I spent several hours working steadily without wanting to be anywhere else. It was exciting. What is happening is that my imagination is engaged; scenes and ideas are filling in the spaces of the story in a satisfying way. I am still not sure of certain things, but I am living with the questions, turning them over in my mind.

AT THE WHITE HOUSE, FOR A RECEPTION GIVEN BY HILLARY CLINTON, WHO SPONSORED THE NATIONAL GEOGRAPHIC BOOK, *SAVING AMERICA'S TREASURES*, IN WHICH I HAD AN ESSAY

The White House was thrilling. Ribboned swags of lacquered fruit and berries framed all the windows. In every corner was another brilliantly decorated tree or a choir singing carols. But the most moving sights were the portraits: Kennedy with his head bowed in thought, Lincoln sitting slightly forward in a chair, Truman staring straight into your eyes. And then the First Ladies portrait room, with Jacqueline Kennedy, Nancy Reagan, and Pat Nixon, her eyes almost unbearably full of pain.

This morning, back in Ashland, I lifted up a narcissus bulb in a teacup on the kitchen windowsill and saw that there was a small bush of new roots on the bottom. Still no visible growth on top, but there is activity and preparation for growth going on. Sometimes, living in Ashland, I feel like a bulb in a teacup, living such a small life.

The notion that we are victims of our own story, that we drag it like a chain mantle behind us, is worth thinking about. We could unclasp the mantle and step away from it if we knew how.

❧

A dream in which I could not get my mother to stop telling people what a slob I was, and in another segment I am being shown by someone else how I have spilled little drops of food on clothes I sent to the cleaners. I was embarrassed and, angry with my mother, I tried to get her attention by dumping a box of stuff on the floor. But nothing worked.

My Christmas story is stalled. Pray for inspiration . . . stay seated.

My old friend P called me from the hospital. A nurse dialed my number, held the phone to his ear. He is in a straitjacket, which he has been in most of his life, but now he is in one literally. What a shock. How sad. His comment: "I thought it was something to help my back. It had a floral print. And I didn't realize until I was in it what had happened." He still retains his humor, but I sensed he was disoriented.

❧

A cold, clear light. The house is quiet. I am in my office, listening to the scratch of my pen and the tick of the clock. Everything I need, including my willingness to remain collected for as long as it takes, is here.

I moved downstairs into the living room and picked up Emerson and his essay, "Spiritual Laws."

The whole course of things goes to teach us faith. We need only obey. There is guidance for each of us, and by lowly listening we shall hear the right word.

Last night, *the right word* came from eight-year-old Alexander Lamm from San Francisco, who came with his parents for dinner. When I told them about the book I was trying to write, Alexander looked at me solemnly and dug into his eight years of experience to say, "A book has to pull you along. It has to be full of inspiration and make you want to do things you hadn't thought of doing before." What good simple advice!

One of the strongest illusions in life is that another person's love will liberate us. The illusion is hard to let go of, even when one Lover after another has disappeared, because while they are present they do set us temporarily "free." We feel as if we are more talented and lovable, and then they turn away and stop loving us, and we realize how much our balloon depended upon their hot air.

2001

When my mother first came to live with me, her eyes were still good enough for her to drive around town, play Scrabble after supper at the kitchen table, and use her Tarot cards as prompts during her morning meditation. But by the end of the first year she could do none of these things, and after giving it some thought she decided—quite uncharacteristically for someone so shy—to create a support group for other people who had macular degeneration. After numerous phone calls and referrals from Kathy Waldroup at Cross Brothers Market, a half-dozen elderly women and several men joined up. I dubbed the group the "Immaculate Degenerates" and the name stuck.

Once a month "the Immaculates" met, usually around our dining room table. Various townspeople volunteered to entertain them. Deering Gaddy gave a lecture on the history of the motorcycle, complete with a video of our local delegate to the state legislature riding around on his Harley. Fan Etienne put on an interactive play. The local llama farm owner walked a few of her llamas down to be petted. And one morning, Lyde Longaker taught everyone how to hand-build clay bowls.

"I think you're finished," dead-panned my mother to her friend Dorothy Jones, who wasn't exactly throwing herself into the project. "In more ways than one," she added.

Some meetings—like the time they learned how to wrap colored string around a pair of chopsticks to make a "God's eye"— were less successful than others. "What is it about making a God's eye that makes me so furious?" Mother whispered. "I feel trapped in it." But word quickly got around town that our dining room was a lively place to be on the first Wednesday of every month, and soon people who could see perfectly well began to show up. Then someone suggested that they meet twice a month. My mother put her foot down.

"I just don't want that much continuity," she said. "I had continuity for forty years. Now I want incontinuity." The once-a-month schedule stayed in place.

Mother's Immaculate Degenerates met yesterday. The subject was Japanese fishing balls. Susan Tucker had written and researched a paper on them for the Women's Club and she had real fishing balls, some of which she bought on eBay to pass around. In the process we were transported around the world, hearing about a Hawaiian island of only pure Hawaiians who make necklaces of littoral, how the invention of mechanized winches scuttled the art of fishing-ball making, and how there is a current that begins in Japan and snakes across the Pacific Ocean, dumping fishing balls on the West Coast beaches of the United States. I was unexpectedly fascinated.

❧

Last night, sitting by the fire, I realized how carefully you have to tend it. No matter how dry the fuel or well-constructed the pyramid of logs and paper, one has to make continual small adjustments—moving the logs closer together or farther apart—to keep the fire going. This is true for relationships as well, although some relationships are easier to keep fired up than others and a few seem very difficult to get going at all.

I have instituted a new custom, of lowering the lights as it gets later, so that by dusk we are sitting in a living room lit only by candles and firelight. It is a gentle, reflective way to finish the day, mimicking the setting of the sun outside.

We ended in a dark living room listening to a meditation tape. My body twitched continually. But mother was as still as a tree. When the tape was over, she opened her eyes, gazed gently around the room, and said, "time for a glass of port and a cig."

I'm grateful for a string of reprieves—from financial worry (a tax rebate), health concerns (weight coming down), and family stress (my children all in good places). Now, dear Lord of Words, fill me with inspiration. My book remains unfinished.

It was probably a mistake to read my work to a friend who did not much like it. This is not to blame my friend, who only did what I asked, which was to listen constructively. What I realize is how easy it is to be rigid or incapable of change. I get it into my head that a story should be one way or that I can't alter it after something is already there. The fact is that I can alter what I want.

A houseguest gone. It was a harmonious visit, but I find it unaccountably hard to like her and continue to wonder why. The closest I can get to it is that there is a kind of shifting, insubstantial quality about her. She does not stand behind what she says if any resistance is offered, which infuriates me.

The only reason to write this down is to see more clearly what lies at the bottom of these reactions. My worry, while she was here, was that she would sense my negativity—the ultimate in inhospitable behavior is to invite someone in and then make her feel uncomfortable.

❦

If I were to die tomorrow, how many messes would I have left behind me that I had run out of time to clean up? More importantly, what kind of shape would I myself be in? What small hardened little heart or large filled-with-love heart would they find?

Last night I lay in bed and felt lost and I cried out silently for help. It is an instinct I had almost lost. There is, instead, a kind of stolid state that resembles sleep. I would rather feel pain.

❦

One of the strongest illusions in life is that another person's love will liberate us. The illusion is hard to let go of, even when one lover after another has disappeared, because while they are present they do set us temporarily "free." We do feel as if we are more talented and lovable, and then they turn away and stop loving us, and we realize how much our balloon depended upon their hot air.

❦

Going into Mother's room to get the Walkman, I see her sitting in her chair, a gray shawl wrapped around her shoulders, her eyes closed in the semidark room. Once again, she has triumphed over the flu and is back in good health. The upright and attentive posture, the waiting, willing pose, sums up someone who loves the truth more than she loves her own will.

I am astray in the world of words and communication. All day yesterday I played at the edge of the ocean—e-mail, letters, phone calls—without ever getting my feet wet. And all because I fear being pulled out to sea without being able to swim.

Yesterday I went through some notes I took of my four-year stint as a writing teacher in an inner-city elementary school in Washington, D.C. Instantly, I am back in the chaos that I was never able to dispel when I was there. Part of it was the school system, which was a disaster, and part of it was me. I lay awake last night thinking about what could possibly be made out of it. My notes are as full of holes as the school, and yet I began to remember specific incidents, like opening up a bank account for a fifth grade student who was trying to save money by sweeping up in a barber shop on Fourteenth Street and how, when the bank checked on my credit, they almost refused to let me co-sign. I return to the feeling that I don't have to admire myself to write about that experience. I just have to be honest without being a victim, since nobody wants or needs a book written by a self-loather.

A gift to myself: Stephen King's book (*On Writing: A Memoir*). He is a hilarious, truthful person, and his book is easy reading. His advice: If you aren't spending about six hours a day, every day, reading and writing, the "guy with the cigar and the bag of magic" won't help you out.

Then I came across this, by the English writer Alan Bennett:

People like me because I'm no threat. They think I'm nice. No writer is nice. It's a misconception. . . . [One is] never wholly dismayed . . . even by tragedy. The awful thing about writing is the eagerness with which you seize on things like that.

It is interesting that Bennett said he doesn't record his feelings in his journal—"They make you wince when you read them"—except perhaps to say "very low" or something similar. "I always wish I had told more lies," he says, "I would write a lot better if I were able to invent myself more than I do. So little happens to me."

All of yesterday was spent cleaning the house. This morning, sitting in my polished lair with Mother's amaryllis dominating the windowsill, I feel polished, too. My contemplation table by the chair has been cleaned out, with the bulk of my books reshelved and only the best (Emerson's essays and Etty Hillesum's *An Interrupted Life*) allowed to remain.

The things I learn are so simple. If you want to love someone better, make room for it—by doing something loving. Yesterday I painted a small wooden recipe box and filled it full of some of my favorite quotations and gave it to my friend

Pat for her birthday. By the time I had finished it, my love for her had grown.

I am in great health, not a single ache or pain, with a clear mind and a calm spirit. Yet I know that the years ahead will demand everything I've got, which may not be enough. When young, we run off an excess of power. As we get older the energy we need and the energy we have equals out. Then it doesn't. We must slow down and finally stop. Journey over.

I am not yet elderly but my life could end now and my death would not be called untimely. After a brief period of mourning, my survivors would go on grinding coffee, scanning the headlines, and rejoicing in their own robust, bone-singing good health, as I do now.

Not long ago I came into the house at dusk. My mother was not there. It was an unsettling sensation. I felt like a six-year-old coming home from school, moving through cold motherless air that did not have an animating principle. Then, convinced that she was just out for a walk, I went upstairs and started to work. Soon, I heard noises in the kitchen, the sound of pots on the stove. I called her name, she answered, and I was as casual about it as if a stock I owned had momentarily dipped and then recovered.

Yesterday, I worked four hours on my Christmas story. I find that reading some of Mary Oliver's poetry enables me to write a few good lines from a place I hadn't found before. Poetry excavates, blasts, cuts through the flab.

Thinking ahead to my birthday tomorrow, I'm not sure any of my children will remember it. Then again, they weren't there when I was born. The impression of my birth upon them is necessarily weaker than their births are on me.

Last night with Dorothy Jones was so restoring. That bird-like, tall thing, bent over a plate she can't see, but so bright and large-hearted. She and Mother are an equal match. Their relationship keeps them both alive.

The best thing to come out of the Immaculate Degenerates was Dorothy Jones, who was totally blind, which didn't keep her from being the hub of the entire Ashland community. I have never known anybody in their nineties who laughed so often, complained so little, and whose phone rang so continually. A retired classics professor, she never married and devoted the last years of her life to caring for her younger, mentally challenged sister, Geezie, in a huge ramshackle ship of a house that was managed by her housekeeper, Esther, who lived in daily terror that Dorothy was going to fire her. "I don't do nothing to earn all this money," she would say. For a while, Esther refused to cash her paychecks. Finally, Dorothy and my mother forced her to drive them to the bank so they could watch her deposit the paychecks in the bank.

Dorothy and my mother quickly became best friends. "Imagine," said my mother, "having a best friend at my age." No two friends could have been more different than my mother, the high school dropout Buddhist transcendentalist who thought the past was something to get over, and Dorothy, who had a PhD, belonged to two Christian churches in town, and whose hobby was family histories. But beneath the surface, they had the same sense of the absurd and a deeply held belief in a life of service. When they took their daily walks with Dorothy's toy poodle, Callie, at the local cemetery, Dorothy would entertain Mother with the stories behind the tombstones. Sometimes, when they passed a newly dug grave, my mother would nudge Dorothy in the ribs and say, "You're next."

Their conversations were worth writing down, and sometimes I did.

MOTHER (after going with Dorothy "to visit the ga-ga" at Crump Manor, one of the more perfect names for an old people's home): It's decided. We've got to get some DO NOT RESUSCITATE bracelets.

DOROTHY (to me): She really got going after she visited Crump.

MOTHER: There's such pathos and history in every room. And you can hear a pin drop, which shows how drugged up they all are.

DOROTHY: Well, we know they're sedated.

MOTHER: Isn't it interesting, the word "sedate." Just add a "d" and you've got "sedated." Did you hear [changing the subject] about the new curbside mortuary viewings in Atlanta? You push a button, and a curtain pulls back so you can see the body and sign the guest book.

DOROTHY: How about the new drive-by sermons in Florida? You just put in a quarter and get the lowdown.

And so on. . . .

As flat and far away from passionate living as I feel, it would still take me quite some time to list the gifts I have been given: my mother, my health, my ongoing financial luck, a cozy house, friends, and permeating all of the above, my children. And so much beauty, from the hills of California to the fog gathering in the fields near Villa Spannocchia in Tuscany.

If I had a wish it would be to have chance and ability to love, not as I used to wish, for a man, although I wouldn't turn a good one down.

A thought comes to me—that what one professes to believe is not always what one actually thinks. Therein lies the disjointedness; energy and resolve drain through the crack between them.

On a mundane level, I think I am capable of swimming half a mile with relative ease. But in the water I don't do it because I feel myself to be weak in resolve. And what I feel is stronger than what I think.

In my writing, I am fearful of risk or change, not because I wouldn't if I could, but because I don't think I can. Here, what I think prevails. Do I have anything to say? In a conversation with my mother, she asked if I knew many wise people. I got to thinking that we all have wisdom, and it is a matter of knowing how to get access to it that makes the difference between us. In speaking with one friend, I am soulful and insightful. With another I can barely complete a sentence. Something in them either produces something in me or doesn't.

❦

Last night I gave myself a birthday dinner and asked people to bring something to share that inspires them. The inspiration-sharing got off to a wonderful start with five-year-old Meade Reihl's drawing, then her seven-year-old brother Alec's story about the trash can snowmen, Magi's favorite book of plants from the southeastern United States, Jeff Reihl's song about "No Time," Cody Artiglia's card, Jesse Artiglia's light-up pen, Pat's poem on "Kindness" by Naomi Shihab Nye, and finally Mel Titus's anecdote about the snow. Yesterday, her eight-year-old son looked up into the sky full of flakes and said, "This is the best day of my life." She said I had that spirit, too. When the cake came and Meade, Jesse, and Cody helped me blow out the candles, I wished for a bigger heart. Second wish: that more people sign up for my seminar in Scotland.

❦

A new thought is like a new footprint in the snow. This is the yield from a morning walk through a snow-filled town.

❦

I am reading *The Leopard* by Giuseppe Tomasi di Lampedusa. It was the only book he ever wrote, and he died shortly after it was published.

Death, oh yes, it existed of course, but it was something that hap-pened to others. The thought occurred to Don Fabrizio that it was inner ignorance of this supreme consolation that makes the young feel sorrows much more sharply than the old; the latter are nearer the safety exit.

It is a beautiful book that consoles the heart and revives the imagination.

While walking around the neighborhood this morning, I passed a house under construction and wondered why humans build such right-angle habitats. Is it because of our skeletal structure, the linear way our minds function? Snails live on a curve, oysters, too. Everything in nature lives in the round except for us. The more I look at our houses, the odder they seem to me.

Yesterday I talked to a wonderful local photographer, Doug Buerlin, about creating a photo essay exhibit called Our Town. He would take the pictures and I would write the commentary. Mother wasn't sure it would be a good idea. "It will get people's noses out of joint if they're not included and their noses are out of joint anyway." I found it lovably unsaintly of her when, later on, she wondered if she had done enough to warrant being included. "I founded the Immaculate Degenerates," she said tentatively.

A manuscript to edit came yesterday, with a check for $500: $250 more came from a magazine for an essay. A writing class starting that will bring $400 a month more. This is serious financial stability. If I activated my Social Security of $820 a month I'd feel quite secure.

In the early eighties I worked as a contract writer at the Washington Post *for several years. The financial stability of a monthly check was wonderful (even though I forgot to put anything aside for taxes—another story), but I didn't feel too inspired sitting at a desk with nothing to look at out the window but another building full of people sitting at their desks across the street. I was also under the impression that working at the* Post *would be like going back to college, with lots of time in the snack bar swapping jokes with my new friends. But everybody kept their heads down and didn't even look up when I walked by. ("That's because everybody's waiting to see if you last long enough to be nice to," said my friend Rudy Maxa, the paper's gossip columnist.) Still, I needed the job because my ex-husband was threatening to sue me for custody of the children and it was important to look respectable. Dick Harwood, the* Post's *deputy managing editor, helped me get hired.*

My old friend and defender at the *Washington Post,* Dick Harwood, is dead. There was a white-hot anger in him that frightened most people, an intensity that was not softened by any of the usual gifts of courtesy or self-deprecation. But he was very honest, and when I asked him about his life he told me a stunning story: his father had been a roustabout in the Wild Bill Hickok Show, he'd seen his mother kill herself and he'd witnessed the death of his sister. Then an orphan, his stingy uncle had taken him in and presented him at the end of his stay with a bill for every nickel he had spent on him. He did not have any self-pity, but I will always remember his voice when he told me about how, at his mother's funeral, "Everyone patted me on the head and said how sad it was but not one of them asked to take me home—not one!"

Dick's funeral at the Navy Chapel in Washington was full of a lifetime of friends and colleagues who came to say good-bye. They were Washington's powerful word and idea people. The familiar faces of Ben Bradlee, Kay Graham, and Walter Pincus were easily picked out. But it was young Helen Harwood, whose face was such a mobile version of her father's, who moved me most. The passion that characterized her father ran freely across her features. Looking at her, I missed him.

Ben's eulogy included the scene of Dick cradling Bobby Kennedy's head on the floor of the LA hotel kitchen after he was assassinated, having to leave him to find a phone to call Ben at the *Post,* then dictating a story "that was poetry," Ben said. There was a stiff and graceful flag ceremony, with gloved hands combing the air, palm out, as the flag was turned into a tricornered packet for Bea, Dick's widow. The marine commander, a chest full of decorative ribbons against dark navy cloth, bending down to deliver his condolences, listening to the pipers play "Amazing Grace."

A funeral is like a train station waiting room. We're all going to board the train someday. Only the schedules vary. In the meantime, we catch up with each other, and assess how we're preparing for the trip. I returned home full of energy and affection.

Mother, sitting by the fire, said, "While there is breath in me, I'll want to stay, as long as there is something more for me to learn, as long as I've got my marbles. If I'm unconscious I don't want a lot of chemicals in me keeping me around for years. That's not right for the body. If I was an Eskimo they'd put me on an ice floe."

My friend Sarah called this morning with two compliments. I didn't know I needed them, but if she had announced she had two hundred, I would have sat as quiet as a mouse while she reeled them all off. The ego is such a hungry creature. I don't now remember what the compliments were, but after they were delivered she recounted a story about her new boyfriend saying to her, "I like your little scalloped scissors." "I can't believe I made out with a man who knows what scalloped scissors are," she exclaimed.

I notice, after going through the diagnostic phase of getting my blood analyzed, teeth examined, and chest X-rayed, that I fall off in interest, and have difficulty taking the next step; filling the prescriptions, taking the thyroid, following the doctor's orders to lose weight. It is as if the diagnosis is enough.

It seems as if my entire life now is revolving around the maintenance of it: teeth, stomach, car, garden, house refinance, piano keys. On the other hand, there is a much greater sense of order that is very comforting, even addicting.

Today is Easter Sunday. On Saturday night, Rose's Department Store was full of people buying plastic toys, gigantic bunny-filled baskets, and cheap fancy dresses for their children to go to church in, but at least there is a slim thread connecting them to the story behind it: "Jesus lives." When I think how quickly we disappear from the face of the Earth when we die, the power of Jesus' life becomes clearer at the checkout counter.

My friend Katy's teenage daughter came for a few minutes to receive her bat mitzvah present from me. A large temple ceremony where the whole community turns out to support one thirteen-year-old girl, at her most awkward, insecure age is a very wise thing. It not only gives her a loving push to the next level but it creates an opportunity for adults—who might otherwise ignore or take a child too lightly—to focus upon her.

This morning I woke up thinking that I may, in some way, be experiencing my mother's life. I feel blind. I cannot seem to see my next creative move. Once again, I read Stephen King's writing memoir: *Tell the truth,* he says. I should try it, really try it. I will write a sentence and then ask, "Is that really true?" or "Can I make it *more* true?"

Mother has some kind of flu bug. She has no symptoms other than a feeling of shakiness and a need for water. I must keep closer to her than usual. Her psychological health, her spirits, need my presence. She needs real care—warm the water, butter the toast—nothing huge, but continual. Her eyes make everything so problematic—the cords of her earphones get tangled, she can't figure out which tape is which. When she went into her closet to get a thermometer, her bathrobe caught on the door and she fell. I am rolling up rugs to create a smoother surface.

I am acutely aware of my mortality now, in a way that is different from my past awareness of it. The beauty and excitement of the world will go on being beautiful and exciting without me. The familiar curves and corners of the towns I love, the voices of my family, the understanding of friends—all of it will pour out of the glass. I wonder if my present quietude is not simply an attempt to make sure I don't run too fast or trip over an excess of feeling. Or is it a reward of age?

❧

Perhaps because I'm trying to hook my writing students on keeping a journal, I'm thinking of them as I write in mine. There are two ways to look at the act of committing your thoughts and feelings to paper:

1. as a frightening revelatory act that leaves you less in control, or

2. as a way of taking your thoughts and fears and subduing them, like pinning butterflies to a wax tablet, so you can examine them more closely.

The second is what has always motivated me.

❧

Looking through an old folder of students' work and my notes about them, I came across a statement uttered by one woman: "No one ever told me I could listen to my heart." The sentence jumped out at me as being so simple and obvious. Yet it is a habit that is so easy to lose, particularly when the inside of one's head is like a crowded restaurant with bad acoustics.

Yesterday there was a late night call from Sarah, who said she thought my lack of strong feelings was a stage or phase. My mother could feel passionately about her life because I was providing her with the safe harbor that enabled her to relax and let her feelings grow.

Mother, speaking about her friend Bessie, whose life is so hard because she is black. The landlord won't look her in the eye, the woman who lives above her takes her handicapped parking space, someone let the air out of her new tires. Mother advises her to send light to the woman. Bessie asks what that means. Mother replies, "It's love," and Bessie says, "I believe I'll try that."

Bessie was one of my mother's long-distance healing clients. I am not the person to explain how long-distance healing works, other than to say that it involves meditating upon specific symbols or archetypes, sending light, and remaining detached from the process. While she was living in California, her spiritual teacher, Lawrence McCafferty, had introduced her to it, and a psychic correctly predicted that she would go to France and work with someone there who had psychic abilities.

After she moved to Ashland, Mom's first client was my cousin's horse, whose ankle had been so badly sprained it would have to be put down if it didn't get better. The ankle improved. Then she was asked by a neighbor to work on his son, who had been in a very bad ski accident. He got well soon afterward. But perhaps the most dramatic example involved my friend Diane, whose son Michael had been suffering from excruciating back problems for years.

When my mother heard about Michael, she asked whether Diane would mind if she tried to heal him from afar. "Of course," she replied gratefully. "I will try to help," said my mother, "but first you must do one thing." When Diane retells this part of the story, she always starts to cry. "What?" she asked. "Get out of the way," said my mother. Michael has not had any back trouble since.

All this work was done behind closed doors in her bedroom, in a wing chair, where she sat quietly and focused her energy and attention upon the person, animal, or situation she had been asked to help. Then one day she announced that she had decided to "go public" with an ad in our local newspaper. "There may be somebody out there I don't know who needs help."

At first the Herald Progress *refused to place the ad, probably because it sounded a little too New Age for its readership. But mother knew Jay Pace, the owner/editor, and when he heard who wanted to place the ad he gave it the go-ahead. The* Herald Progress *didn't have a* HEALING *category but agreed to make one. "It's Category Thirty-six," she exclaimed happily, "between* HAY *and* HELP WANTED. *Three and six add up to nine, which is the Tarot card with the magician holding up his lantern to give light—which is what it's all about—even if no one calls."*

The ad was straightforward, offering telephone consultation for people who were suffering from physical or mental distress, although my mother wanted to make sure that people didn't think she was a born-again Christian. ("I added 'trained by a European healer' to lift it out of the Pentecostal business.") Then she sat back and waited for the phone to ring.

The first caller was a man who said he was having trouble with his prostate gland. Mother was somewhat taken aback, and it took her a few minutes to realize that he was an obscene caller. "When he asked me how old I was, I realized he just wanted a little sex chat. After I told him I was eighty-four, he hung up."

All told, perhaps several dozen readers saw my mother's ad and phoned for help. Some of them, like Bessie and her son, William, became dear friends. There was no charge, but every so often an envelope appeared in the mail, with a couple of dollars and a thank-you note inside.

The other morning I went walking through the woods beyond De Jarnette Park. Moving along the path, my face was brushed by spider threads that broke as I walked. Only the first walker of the morning would ruin the spider's plan. Moral: don't cast your ideas too low across the path if you want them to survive.

Ashland was as cool and fragrant as a Mull morning. The leaves, now fully out on all the trees, overlapped each other, filtering the light. Tiny birds rolled off the leaves, like plump drops of water, onto the grass and flew up into the branches again.

Walking home, down England Street, past all the flags that Virginians love to hang outside their houses, I saw them in a more positive light, as stained-glass windows that the sun illuminated. Granted, the sun was lighting up appliquéd flowers, bunnies, and Virginia Tech symbols, but still I saw the similarities between them and the windows in Chartres. The whole world is a stained-glass window and you don't have to be on an island in Scotland or in a hill town in Italy to see it.

❧

When we say negative things about ourselves we are really trying them on for size, to see if we really believe our own words. Yesterday, for example, I was talking to my sister, Cynthia, on the phone and said, "I am always pining to be someplace better than here." And she said, "Yes, you do that a lot, don't you?" I didn't appreciate the confirmation even though she was only agreeing with what I had just said.

❧

IN SAN FRANCISCO FOR THE WEEKEND BEFORE HEADING UP TO THE BISHOP'S RANCH IN HEALDSBURG FOR MY SEMINAR

Why do we take the place we were born so personally? What is it in our natures that makes us consider the streets and trees, the very light itself where we grew up as sacred and empowering? I am not sure, but whenever I am in California I feel like a grandee who looks upon everything as my inheritance or dowry. California is my trust fund, one that I can never deplete.

I went with a friend to Crissy Field, a newly created marsh and beach along San Francisco Bay. Sitting on the beach, I watched kites, wind surfers, and yachts leaning close to the water. In the distance, huge tankers nearly blotted out Marin County.

There are changes. Presidio Terrace where my aunt and uncle used to live is closed to traffic. A uniformed guard by the gate outside of Senator Diane Feinstein's house blocked our way. We speculated that the Palestinian-Israeli terrorism attacks were the reason. A sidewalk sale on nearby Lake Street made me feel rooted. I bought a $5 tablecloth and felt at home.

Until this trip I had never ventured inside Temple Emanu-el, whose orange tiled dome had dominated my childhood neighborhood. It is a formal place of prayer, with a large courtyard and deep interior worship space flanked by green marble columns. Along one wall is a large stained-glass window with strands of brilliantly colored glass flowing across the face of it. From the street, you cannot appreciate its beauty. But from inside the sanctuary, Temple Emanu-el blazes with light.

AT THE BISHOP'S RANCH SEMINAR

During our first evening together, we go around the circle to introduce ourselves. I am struck by the way the introductions begin where they should and end where they must. I chose to start with Pat, who said she would have frozen if she'd had any time to think. She broke the ice by saying that she wasn't a writer but was "just Pat." This gave everyone permission to be themselves without feeling the need to pad or promote a résumé.

Bev was eloquent about her hospice work, where she sees the innocence and openness of a child return to the people who are dying and want to tell her their secrets because they know that she will keep them.

Jill was the last to speak—and she was heartbreakingly direct. "I'm the most self-centered person here," she began. "I want to see if I can feel anything at this late date." She spoke about how she has begun to wake up earlier and earlier, "Before I can make trouble for myself or anyone else," and just being with herself for what her mother used to call "added minutes," when one got to spend unexpected time with someone.

The ranch house is full of good books, which is like being surrounded by good people, Ken Wilber next to Jacob Needleman, for example. Books need no towels or linen, just an inch on a shelf. And they'll talk to anybody who will listen.

"Fame in this country is a religion that demands human sacrifice," writes Wilber [in One Taste]. *"You end up exactly with what Oscar Levant said to George Gershwin: 'Tell me, George, if you had to do it all over again, would you still fall in love with yourself?'"*

THE NEXT DAY

The ship is under sail, as I had hoped it would be by now, with some real writing beginning to emerge. I find these women very nourishing and, in short, fine, or finely wrought: Mimma, sitting for long hours at a table on the porch, relishing the uninterrupted peace to think and express herself, away from a very sick husband; Marge, bearing the cross of her two dead sons and trying so hard to carry it.

Jeanne's poems are gentle and accessible:

> *each holy thing is borrowed,*
> *everything depends.*

Those last two words fit so effortlessly together, as if they have been headed toward each other since birth.

Lois, eighty-seven, carries a tumor on her kidney and a large cardboard box with her autobiography in it in her arms. Her small birdlike face is beautiful. I told her she had a fine mind, and her eyes filled with tears. "Since my stroke I cry more easily."

Last night, watching Nancy Hiles sit on the floor creating an ikebana flower arrangement, was like meditating. Nancy was entirely wrapped up in the process, delicately cutting a leaf here, a leaf there, so that the end effect—a few sprays of bamboo and a yellow lily rising from a mound of stones in a blue bowl—was perfect. This was the most unusual thing I had done in a long time: sitting in a circle, silently watching someone arrange flowers. No one moved.

The final morning

The cool fog-filled air begins the day as it has every day. By nine-thirty, when we sit down at the table to write, it is almost gone. There is something too factual about midday. There are no shadows to give things a deeper meaning. But in the early morning and late afternoon, the "hour of gold," which Anne Morrow Lindbergh writes about, returns.

Last night as we sat for the last time together, I allowed the reality we had created between us to make itself felt. I realized what I always realize when I'm in the midst of one of these seminars—that my hunger to feel whole has been fed.

Back in Ashland with a new group of writers, I spoke of Emerson and then read them the first paragraph from his great essay, "Self-Reliance."

To believe your own thought, to believe that what is true for you in your private heart is true for all men——that is genius.

They were amazed at his clarity. How did he come to such authority? one of them asked. "He chose his life early," was my answer. Most of us don't, or we wait until we are much older and must correct our course.

After an operation for a basal cell cancer on her face, Mother is zonked out on Demerol. "You can't know how much I deserve this," she muttered, half asleep. Today I will stick very close.

Parallel lists in my journal today make me smile at how divided I am. At the top of one list I wrote COST SAVERS, after which I wrote *change phone companies, use clothesline, walk more, drive less, shop wisely, consume less.* The other list is labeled TODAY. Beneath it I wrote *Send house present of silver coffeepot to Moira* and *Get hair appointment at Blondie's.*

To go to bed thinking about the little dreams and obstacles that are in my life and to wake up with these same small obscuring preoccupations in my mind: How can I spend my precious life squandering it this way? Do I think I will live forever? Am I waiting for some large catalyzing event or realization to show me the way? Not consciously, but this morning I said again, "You have not written anything significant for almost a year." This is the truth I must face. And the second truth is that I am out of money again.

Last evening, at an Ashland party in a noisy house full of people I didn't know, I found a quiet place on the side porch and sat there with the host's dog, listening to the rain come through the trees.

I thought about how most of us are asleep while waking, how we open and shut our mouths making conversation, but we are still asleep. Perhaps the only difference between them and me is that I *know* I'm asleep. Then, not wanting to appear rude, I returned to the party and had an unexpectedly interesting conversation with someone who has been meditating for twenty years, is taking a natural health correspondence course, and could not be less asleep.

Yesterday I felt a deeper, more definite obligation to be a daily, even hourly, caretaker for my mother. I had gone to Washington for the night. To be in a pretty living room talking to smart people about events and ideas that are rarely taken out of the closet in Ashland was a relief. But returning I found that Mother had mistakenly ripped off the bandage on her leg. A pile of dry oatmeal had spilled out of the box onto the floor, and she hadn't seen it. I am needed here. Somehow, I will have to dig down for my stimulation instead of leaving town. I have no access to new ideas this morning, but there is a deeply felt care and connectedness to my life, a sense that it is wide and deep.

One of the ways I keep my books from flying into hiding is to alphabetize them. The wing chair where I sit in the morning is just below the L section, so I am unusually familiar with books by Joseph Lash, Laurie Lee, and C. S. Lewis, whom I plucked off the shelf a minute ago. Like all good writers, Lewis is simultaneously simple and suspenseful:

As I left the railway station at Worchester and set out on the three-mile walk to Ransom's cottage, I reflected that no one on the platform could possibly guess the truth about the man I was going to visit.
—The opening sentence of Perelandra

IN CALIFORNIA: BIG CREEK

I am at the Farr's cabin in Big Sur, sitting on a rock by the rushing creek as it pours down from the mountain. All night its gentle roar was just a few feet away. This place has been treated kindly by the human beings who have lived here. There are only a few cabins, a hammock, and a suspension bridge. Last night I listened to Belinda Holliday tell me about the death of her son, Kenneth, when he was ten. She knew somehow that he would not have a long life, and his death precipitated her career as a plein air painter. Painting, she said, was something she could do that didn't remind her of him.

Later, I hiked down to the beach where the fresh water meets the salt beneath the massive Big Creek Bridge. There were at least a hundred western gulls resting on the sand. Red-tailed hawks wheeled above, and then a pair of oystercatchers—shiny black birds with long pincer-shaped red beaks like a pair of chopsticks—arrived. The beach is full of a kind of natural jade that is plentiful here. One piece will return home with me. It sits solidly on my lap and has a soft, slippery feeling to it.

Looking at a huge boulder nearby, I realize that shifts in power are going on all the time, yet the largest ones are so slow in happening we don't realize it until the transfer is complete. That boulder had made its way down the side of a mountain and the length of a creek bed before coming to rest on this beach by the Pacific. It has been on the beach for a long time. But it took an equally long time to get there.

The difference between the twenty-five-year-old who sat in jeans and a straw hat on a boulder in Big Creek and the sixty-two-year-old who visited that same creek today is an internal emptiness that lets the creek in. There is so much more room inside, as if the many selves and fears that used to compete for space have coalesced or disappeared so that now I am almost a bystander in my own life.

Later in the afternoon all the Farr's guests got in a van, drove to the top of a ridge, and sat in Jeffers's "windy company of the grasses," looking out to the sea. Behind us were mountains, humped, ridge-backed, and wrinkled, straw-colored beneath blue sky. I couldn't get enough of it.

Rereading an earlier part of my journal, I came across the lines where I say that Emerson chose his life early. I have chosen to be a writer and must be willing to do what it takes. It is like drilling for oil, having the faith that it is down there. But beyond or beneath that faith is the commitment to dig, whether the oil is there or not.

Before going to bed last night I read an interview with Larry Dossey on the efficacy of prayer. The image that comes to my mind when I think of somebody praying is of a fisherman mending his nets, each intersection of the net being a soul that is part of the whole. He goes from one to the other, examining, repairing, strengthening them.

Sitting in a semidark living room in the early morning, I look at a black-and-white photograph and wait for the light to transform it. It is an amazing daily occurrence, going from black and white to color. Is this the difference between the enlightened and unenlightened mind?

☙

Mom's ninety-year-old friend, Dorothy Jones, is in the hospital with a broken hip. She lay in the driveway behind her house for an hour before she was found. An unfeeling doctor told her she would never be able to put on her own underwear again. So there she lies, trying not to be depressed. What was he *thinking*?

Standing in the kitchen, I thought of all my friends and their burdens: sickness, loneliness, children who won't talk to them. All the protective circles we try to construct around ourselves are illusions or, more accurately, are temporary and do not hold.

☙

Last night, I had dinner in Richmond, Virginia, with some friends who live in a Gatsby-like pile of stone with endless rooms impeccably furnished, surrounded by rolling lawns, ivy-covered walls. "You must feel like you're in a movie," I said to the husband. "At first it was daunting," he confessed.

Although I have no desire to be part of that world, something pleasant tugs at me when I drive through neighborhoods full of massive oaks, brushed velvet lawns, and fortress-like mansions. I passed a couple of young teenagers in shorts leaning against a parked car. They seemed wrapped in privilege, staring at me through layers of protection that they wore as casually as their own skins.

This morning I awoke with a prayer: "Help me to have the courage to finish what I have begun and to begin what I want to finish."

What needs to be recorded is my widening belief in personal prayer. For not very long I have tried to go to bed each night praying for different people I love. Last week, prayers were answered. I don't know why this new conviction, that there is a connection between my prayers and prayers being answered, but it has descended upon me like a cloak around my shoulders that the prayers I send and the improvement I witness are joined.

Reading Emerson "On Virtue"—which he distrusts—I think that by and large I am not virtuous. But I would say that I am susceptible to and appreciative of people who are virtuous and wish to be like them. But crossing the room, so to speak, is difficult. I just stand on my side admiring what could, by imitating them, be mine.

Yesterday, on the tennis court, I battled to remember that I was in Ashland, not Monterey, playing tennis with Mother's friend Reber, not my brother Tony. The imagination always wants to "digitally enhance" reality, make it easier and more entertaining to be alive. But I knew the truth was better and tried to stay with it.

One thing I notice is that when I fall behind in a tennis game, I give up. Reber pointed this out to me some time ago, and he is right. I want so much to win that when I'm not doing well I lose heart and want to stop. The vigor to persist leaves me. Where does this lack of confidence come from? And how can I punch through it?

On writing, I wonder if I am now a shade tree for younger writers rather than a fruit-bearing tree myself. But how would I know? It's like wondering if I am an athlete when I stay indoors.

It is dangerous to ask questions if you're not prepared to accept the answers. I asked Mother whether I had a short attention span. "Yes," she said, "except when you're writing. You focus for a moment, but then it's gone, so that many mundane things go by the board. You've got so much going on in your head."

Then the question I don't ask: Do I share what's going on inside my head? It seems to me that the larger the concern, the smaller is my instinct to divulge it—out of a desire to control the outcome.

Another question to myself: Am I learning anything new, putting myself in new situations, or staying in the same familiar "rooms" I've been in for so long? Do we fool ourselves into thinking that we are going into new territory? Last night I sat quietly in the living room after supper and read my friend Jean Emerson's poetry from her latest chapbook, *Cycles of the Moon Vine*. She answered the last question for me.

> *We smile beneath our constant worries*
> *We cherish our obligations.*
> *They shelter us*
> *From the howling emptiness*
> *   of possibility*
> *From our responsibility*
> *to recognize our own reality.*

Later, in bed, I read an interview with a man trying to wean us away from the advertising culture. Everything is a billboard, he said, even the clouds. (IBM recently put a laser image of its logo on a cloud in San Francisco.) It is true. We are inundated with messages and consider reading a J. Crew catalog intellectual activity. I personally read three last night—a summer sale catalog, a regular-price catalog, and another I don't remember—thereby wasting for all eternity fifteen minutes.

I had a strange thought this morning. If I were to imagine myself walking through the upper floor of a large house with different parts of myself in different rooms, which door would I be afraid to open, what self would I be afraid to meet?

The self I would be afraid to meet would be the self I had neglected. She is the self who gets pushed aside by the optimistic, practical, reality-denying self who moves in front to protect and deny the self who might otherwise pull everything down.

But now, after years of keeping that neglected self at bay, I miss her. She is my heart, and only when I am in a position of command do I let her in to guide me. When I'm teaching, she is there: advising a friend, comforting a child, any area where I am dealing from strength. But that strong part is, for the most part, unsoftened by tears. I won't let her cry in front of me. So she doesn't, except when taken by surprise.

The self behind the door I am afraid to open is the self who had her innocence taken away from her, who longed to be loved by her husband but was criticized and cuckolded instead. She lived in fear that something horrible would happen to one of her children, that she would die of terror not knowing where they were. Lost, wailing, trapped, in wet diapers behind crib bars, they would be weeping for their mother and I would not be there.

Jeanne Moreau's interview on *60 Minutes* with Mike Wallace struck me hard. When Wallace asked her if she thought it was true that women of a certain age should be done with passion, she nodded. "It's true what they say," she replied. "With passion you are up and down. Love is steady, even."

❧

Yesterday I received a rejection letter from *Hope* magazine (which strikes me as a funny fact). They had torn off the return address from my letter and taped it to their envelope, which contained an unsigned form letter.

This is the first rejection letter I've gotten since the late sixties, when I used to send out old stuff and get it back quick as a boomerang. Well, I was sending out old things again, albeit previously published, so perhaps there is a lesson to be learned. But I decided not to let the feeling of rejection demonize the rejecter, who is probably a very bright well-meaning junior editor sitting in front of a huge stack of unsolicited manuscripts.

Then, at racquetball a little later, my partner commented on how well I was playing. I said I had gotten a rejection letter that afternoon and was probably profiting from the sense that I didn't have anything more to lose. The ego should be monitored like an automobile tire—not too full, not too empty.

❧

IN WILLIAMSTOWN, MASSACHUSETTS, TO SEE [MY YOUNGER SON] JUSTIN, IN A PLAY

Just writing down the name of the play, *Observe the Sons of Ulster, Marching Toward the Somme,* brings tears to my eyes.When he stepped onto the stage into that pool of bright gold light, my heart was stunned by his truthfulness, the command and sharpness of his presence. And in the end, when he prayed for his men, so soft and cherishable going to the slaughter, I wept again.

Now I am home, nursing an ache that is at least partially an ache for my own youth—longing to be thirty again, surrounded by other thirty-year-olds who are so bright, clever, and beautiful. "Accept your place on the conveyor belt," I say to myself. There is nothing so unattractive as someone trying to run backward. But the sadness that we will never be on the same portion of the belt, that one day I will be dumped off it, remains.

This morning, as I woke up and got dressed, I found myself searching in my mind for friends, the way I search my closet for clothes. Who are they? How many do I have? We live in a world of shifting affections, mine as well as others, but it seems to me that to relate to myself in such a lateral way, taking my measure by how others weigh me, is false. I must go inside, where my ability to relate to life is not dependent upon who relates to me, and take my own internal soundings.

Yesterday, sixteen-year-old Miranda Longaker came to visit. She brought her flute and played it for me—very well. Then she asked me how my writing was going, and I told her the synopsis of my Christmas story so far. I confessed to being stuck. "You can't give up on it," she said. "Just start in a new place if you're stuck in the old one."

❦

SEPTEMBER 11, 2001

[journal empty.]

SEPTEMBER 12, 2001

Yesterday, America's whole world changed when we were attacked by terrorists who hijacked four commercial jets, flew two of them directly into the World Trade Center towers—which collapsed with thousands of people inside—another into the side of the Pentagon, and a fourth, destined for Camp David, into the ground.

It began at 8:45 A.M. Minutes before, I had been downstairs in the kitchen, listening to the radio and its daily sadness. Shimon Peres and Yasser Arafat couldn't agree on a place to meet for peace talks. I said to Mother, "The world is so sick." She agreed. And then, minutes later, the first plane struck the World Trade Center tower. I was upstairs in my office. The phone rang and my friend Pat said, "Turn on your television." The country watched as the second plane approached and struck the second tower. Within less than two hours both of them had fallen to the earth, and the skyline was empty where once they had been. The shock waves will be endless.

All commercial travel has been halted. The president got on the air and made a brief, not particularly forceful statement that terrorists and the countries that hide them will not be tolerated. But he is clearly in shock, too. This is the first time in my life that the bubble of protection has been shattered, that my capacity for happiness has been radically altered from the outside. We are at war, but the enemy is unlabeled, and I pray that we don't go on a shooting spree that plunges the entire world into darkness.

I dread opening a newspaper or turning on the television. And I pray that every person killed was instantly plucked by an angel into the next world.

∽

September 13, 2001

At eleven-thirty last night, Justin called on his cell phone from New York City. He had been working in Toronto but managed to rent a car and get back to the city, where he returned it and tried to take a cab to his apartment. But the driver wouldn't take him any farther than Fourteenth Street. As he walked down an empty Manhattan street pulling his suitcase behind him, the air was full of smoke. He could not believe what he was seeing—all the thousands of New Yorkers beneath the rubble, a five-story crematorium. The image of a young man dragging his suitcase behind him on a dark deserted street, horrified and awestruck over the desolation, remains with me.

Bill Moyers on television the other night, trying to sort out the horror of the last days, said, "I don't believe that life has meaning. I believe that we *give* life meaning." Yes, this is what I believe, too, that every moment is a moment of choice, whether to invest our lives with significance and love or not.

Images: the wrecked sections of the World Trade Center lying like jagged shards of a cathedral on the rubble. The way the dust has soaked the air in a white bath. There is no color. The light cannot penetrate the dust. New York is a city covered with pictures. Find this man. Help me find this woman. Who has seen, or knows, where he, she, is.

෴

SEPTEMBER 16, 2001

Justin at La Guardia, waiting in line to check in for a flight to Los Angeles. He sounds solemn but calm. We talked about living in the present, embracing fear and then detaching from it. I told him he was in God's hands, that I felt he would be fine. He said he needed to keep doing what he did for a living, because to stay put would be to cycle between depression and fear. I asked him to repeat for me the prayer he always says before he goes onstage so I could write it down. ("God, remove my fear and direct my attention toward what You would have me be.")

Thinking about how our country was taken unawares by the terrorists, how we had no idea that we were going to be attacked, reminds us that the demand for human intelligence depends upon human community. This is where America is primitive and the third world is sophisticated. We are a nation of isolated people, living in planned communities slashed by six-lane highways. We do not know who our neighbors are.

My mother's cigarette man in Ashland is an Arab who lost six friends in the World Trade Center. She asked me to drive her to the local florist, where she bought six red roses in a vase, and then we drove them over to Kassam. He saw us park, and when I walked in with the flowers he knew what they were for and from whom. He had already put a carton of Mom's favorite American Spirit cigarettes into a bag and pushed them toward me—a gift. "You never know," he kept saying, about his dead friends. "You never know." I told him how sorry I was and put my arms around him. It was such a small little piece of thread, but my mother had seen it, blind as she is, and plucked it off the ground. We must be looking out *for* each other, not *at* each other, to make these connections.

❧

In Italy

Sitting once again in Villa Spannocchia's living room, a fire burning quietly, a pitcher of purple wildflowers on a wooden table, bright morning light coming through the shutters.

Spannocchia is at its most beautiful this time of year. A light dew covers the lawn, the orange geraniums in earth-colored pots are sharp against the blue sky. Walking up the hill this morning toward the pigpens, I turned around and saw the tower swathed in fog, the cypress trees framing it at the base. Yesterday we went down to the vineyards and picked grapes. By evening they were pressed and heaps of skins lay in the *fattoria* courtyard, red plastic buckets rinsed and ready for new service today.

Back at the villa, I found the artist Anne Truitt's journal, *Turn,* in the bookcase. On her father, she writes:

It never, I think, occurred naturally to him that the kernel of a human being is divine.

On making the right choice:

The hallmark of a decision in line with one's character is ease and contentment, and an ample, even provision of natural energy.

On aging:

I have come face-to-face with age itself. Inelasticity. An unrelenting wall of physical weakness that no amount of willpower denied. I could not have done more. And no spring of energy rose in me as it did only five months ago when I caught Charlie at the beach. I am not exactly ashamed. That would be silly. I am changed. Irreversibly changed.

Truitt is a light to read by.

❧

Last night I took my writers to a nearby convent for a vespers service. I never tire of looking at those Italian nuns, most of them quite young, sitting sideways to the altar. Their faces, gazing down at their missals, are as still as ponds while their fingers methodically replace the ribbon markers on a new page as they move through the service. I thought how safe they are, many centuries away from the world we live in, with planes crashing into skyscrapers and people afraid to get a hamburger in a Siena McDonald's.

Our last complete day at Spannocchia

The papers are full of terrorism—anthrax, the FBI bungling. All of us fly back to the United States next week. Despite the dangers there, as opposed to the peace here, I am more comfortable at home.

In front of me outside the villa living room window is the beauty I never tire of: lawn, stone walls, cypress trees, and the rolling hills beyond. Other little notes in the margin: wood smoke, doves cooing, *nipitella* mint in the grass. Last night, walking down the hill from the restaurant in Orgia, the sky was thick with stars. My friend Jennifer Storey and I gossiped quietly about some of the villagers: Eve and Vittorio, always with their eye on the main chance, don't sit well with the other villagers; Nina and Federico have erected a gate to keep out Eve and Vittorio's marauding cats. Beneath the stars we think pretty small, but perhaps it keeps us from being overwhelmed.

At Jennifer's house, I had a chance conversation with a Portuguese man, sixty-six, who said he had recently finished translating Saint Teresa of Avila's *Interior Castle*. I asked him if the experience had changed him. No, he said, but he had concluded that her mystical experiences were true visions, not the work of the devil or the hysterical thoughts of an over-heated female mind. "They have the hallmarks of true love as I have experienced it," he said. I asked him what he meant. He said that the experience opened her heart to others, deepened her compassion, inspired her to be of greater service. "This is part of my experience, too."

The trip to the Uffizi in Florence was unsatisfying this time. The headsets were difficult to work, the treatment of the rooms cursory, and none of the guides knew how to find Ghirlandaio, my favorite Renaissance painter. So after an hour of traipsing distractedly through rooms full of masterpieces, I emerged outside into the long alley that runs between the two gallery wings. Suddenly, I heard the most angelic soprano voice singing "Ave Maria." There, standing by an open guitar case, was a young woman singing with such purity and passion that my eyes filled with tears. There is so much beauty in Florence, yet it took a real experience, a flesh and blood girl singing her heart out, to move my own.

❧

A conversation with Jennifer that I've been meaning to record. We had been talking about feeling locked, or trapped, in our lives. Jennifer remarked that when this occurs in her she knows, on some level, how to unlock the door, how to free herself. The solution, or key, is right there, on the table, so to speak. But she doesn't want to use it. She ignores it.

Back in Ashland with winter coming on, the trees racing with color and the sky bright blue. Dorothy Jones's younger brother, Hunter, died last week. He was eighty-two. The Jones family has been in their best clothes ever since, as the town comes to call upon them. I am one of the first, signing my name beneath some of the community's aristocrats, Jim Pollard, Susan and Woody Tucker, people who form the "long bones" of the town.

Mother remarked that Dorothy might not last too much longer. She had said to Mother, "What will I do without H?" as she calls him. "Well, perhaps you will decide you don't want to live without him and that will be that. You can relax." Mom hasn't actually said this to her but thinks she will.

At Hunter's funeral, fully one half of the church was reserved for his family. They came walking down the aisle, at least fifty sons, daughters, grandchildren, and cousins, tears streaming down their cheeks. It is a Jones characteristic that everyone knows about: they cry easily. The rest of the church was crammed with friends who cared deeply, fiercely, about Hunter. He had put so many of them on their feet, helped them out, encouraged them.

I thought sadly of another Ashlander who had died a few days earlier under far different circumstances. A former mayor, overwhelmed by chronic depression, had left notes for his family, driven out of town, and hanged himself from a tree near the railroad tracks. He, too, had his admirers, of whom I was one.

∾

A visit last night from the Nickersons from Maine. Fran is a woman of such enthusiasm and affection; Guy, at seventy-nine, a man you want in your life, quietly replacing the molding on a window, fixing the lock on a door. Fran, in particular, has never been happier, in love with learning, with Senior College, her poets, and art history. "I had to miss the Enlightenment to come here," she said, "and Elizabeth Bishop, about whom I know nothing. But I'll get back in time for Langston Hughes and T. S. Eliot."

We sat in the living room, and I read them Thurber's "Greatest Man in the World." Then Guy read Thurber's "The Bear Who Could Take It or Leave It Alone."

I relished the preterrorist feeling of comfort the Nickersons created: the quiet talk about Maine writers, Guy replacing my rain gutters, and how they feel insulated in Maine from what is going on elsewhere.

Holding a mug of warm coffee to my chest, which is covered in a clean Egyptian flannel nightgown, I wonder if I could even have a thought without these supports? My body's every signal—warm me, cool me, rest me, feed me—is my command.

Weaker signals—exercise me, floss me, hydrate me—involve a higher degree of discipline and formal thinking. The slave doesn't move so quickly to answer these requests, perhaps because he senses that they are not a priority. He can let them slide without losing his job.

Report from the West: my brother John—who moved to Sequim, Washington this year—pulled an eighteen-pound silver salmon from the river behind his new house. After all the struggles he has gone through in his life, there is something shining and triumphant about that.

Mom is getting funnier. She joked yesterday about going to the cemetery with Dorothy ("We go there because no one talks back") to walk Dorothy's dog, Callie. "The big shots get the big tombstones, just like in life," she said.

"I've been thinking," she continued, "that I don't want you to bury my ashes anywhere. It's ridiculous to think about going all the way up to Angel's farm and then you have to stop off at McDonald's for lunch and you have to leave me in the car or bring me inside in a box. No, just forget about the ashes."

A message from the ground was delivered yesterday morning as I took my walk along the wooded path that borders the Randolph-Macon College playing fields. While thinking that I had probably played my last game of tennis and would have to fall back upon walking as my principal form of exercise, my left foot caught upon something in the path and I went abruptly down for the count. Picking myself up, I retraced my steps to see what it was that had caught my foot and found a thick loop of a tree root, too tough to pull up, hidden beneath the leaves.

Today, with the public interest in my mind and a hacksaw in my hand, I went back to saw the root off so others won't be hurt. But the primary thought that came to me is that there is no real certainty that the next moment will be available to us. A tree root could permanently alter one's future. A plane could fly into a skyscraper, anthrax be inhaled from an envelope.

The terrorists have sobered and scared everyone. But all the talk is about how to defend ourselves or kill the perpetrators and none about how to create a society that renders terrorism moot.

An exchange with my new friend, the writer George Crane, who said that writing was his practice, his meditation, the means by which he felt whole and grounded. "It's your way in," I commented. "Yes," he said, "it's my way in." So it is for me.

Last night I did not sleep—acid reflux, even with an expensive $4 pill, which conspired to make me very anxious about my financial future. Here we are, going into a terrible decline with fewer and fewer jobs, I am without any reliable source of income, with new expensive bills for medical problems, and I am on the verge of going into debt. To avoid this I will liquidate my stock portfolio if I can and try to remain outside the equity line. But I do not see any give anywhere.

Rarely do I consult my soul without a prop, like this pen and journal, which simultaneously obscures and preserves what emanates from within. Throughout the day, I am almost always accompanied by another voice—from a radio, magazine, phone, or newspaper.

When the desire is strong enough, talent shows up, like a day laborer, to help you achieve your goal.

This is the line I labored over most of the morning, and it felt deeply satisfying to see it on the page. It is the answer to the question, How do you acquire a belief in oneself, how do you overcome powerlessness of any kind?

Writing is a bit like swimming in the ocean. You have to get beyond the wave line into the depths. But the fear of not getting back to shore, of drifting out to sea, can make the swimmer/writer panic.

Yesterday I paid bills, taking the last bits of money from my business account that can be called mine and paying the mortgage through December. Then the other, smaller bills were addressed. I feel oddly as if I am closer to nature now, like a plant dependent on roots and rainfall, and there is no sense in becoming anxious. Still, if I did not have any recourse—a mother with some ability to help, the future of my teaching, Social Security coming in March—I might not be quite so sanguine.

❧

Finding inspiration where and when I can—this time in the bathtub—from Gary Zukav in *O: The Oprah Magazine*. He writes that we must be conscious of our intentions because who we are and the life we lead is directed and shaped by them.

How hard it is to catch the drift of one's own thoughts or life. But Emerson is always an anchor. His words are clean and clear, giving me hope.

Love and you shall be loved.

A great man is always willing to be little. Whilst he sits on the cushion of advantages, he goes to sleep.

I have been thinking that I have failed the test of love; I do not have anyone whom I really love on a daily basis. But then I remember my mother and adjust my grade from a D to a B minus, even though it is I who feels loved by her.

❧

Mother is beginning to see spirits. "I'm not seeing at all well, but I'm seeing inner things, and then there's all this purple." She described it as a kind of radiant saturation or aura that surrounds what she sees.

"Over the last year I've been having figures coming into my meditation. They are souls who want you to help them. You bless them and say, 'I'm not the one.'"

Yesterday she saw me coming into the house, and five feet behind me was a blonde-haired woman in a quilted down coat. "She would have come right in if I hadn't told her to leave." My sister, Cynthia, who is visiting from California, and I both thought of the same person. "I wonder if it was Barbara [my best friend in college, who died when she was fifty-one]," I said. Mother immediately felt this was right. "If I thought that it was Barbara, I wouldn't have told her to go away."

At the cemetery yesterday, she saw two ghost children coming running toward her. They were about twenty yards away, a twelve-year-old girl and a younger brother, holding hands, and then a woman. "I shined them off," she said, in all seriousness. "It was just too much, with Callie running all over the place and Dorothy bumping into tombstones, and then Cynthia slipped on her crutches, almost falling into a new grave."

For someone whose entire life revolved around the spiritual world, Mother was surprisingly unmoved by the spirits themselves. They weren't her responsibility and she considered them a supernatural nuisance, gray ghosts who cluttered up the supermarket aisles and made it difficult for her to find the produce section without staring at the floor for guidance. But most of the time she lived with them the way other people live with floaters in their peripheral vision—without complaint or comment.

I woke up with financial worries on my mind, not so oppressive as to cripple me but just there, like a reality I must deal with as best I can.

What is the difference between hope and dependence? The first is grounded in the belief in certain truths that will support you if followed. The other relies upon someone or something else to open the door one stands before.

❧

Yesterday, Cynthia and I went to a reception at artist Nancy Witt's house. My feelings were hurt rather effectively by a man who was attracted to Cynthia and made it clear to me that he thought I was old and unattractive. "God's joy moves from box to box," said Rumi. So does God's pain.

It is always harder, I think, to have something and then lose it. Fame, privilege, wealth, physical beauty, love. Yet when you look at these words on a written line, they are not assets that the people I admire or try to emulate possess except secondarily.

Winter is coming. The few brightly colored leaves remaining on the trees are more noticeable because of the spaces created by the leaves lying on the ground. Winter subtracts and creates beauty that is just as compelling as spring, which adds it back.

❧

Yesterday I worked on my book (which finally has a proper name, *Giovanni's Light*), but I did not move forward. Rather, I fiddled with what I'd already written and didn't break new ground. It is an old impulse, rooted in the desire to create a perfect piece of something before moving on—as if the light of what I have created will show me where to go next.

It has been a rough few days, assailed by both financial and creative worries. This week I must liquidate some assets to pay my bills. I am approaching the bottom of the bucket financially.

Now I have an entire outline, chapter by chapter, of *Giovanni's Light*. It gives me a box in which to put the contents. Afterward, I celebrated by running out to Campbell's Ceramics and buying some clay, firing cones, and other equipment.

Some years ago, I bought a block of clay at a garage sale and discovered the joy of kneading a jug or face or small earthen figure into existence with my fingers. Like making quilts, another hobby I pursue with joyous inexactitude, playing with clay satisfies a need to feel the material world between my hands after so many hours in the abstract world of words.

Reading Emerson, I came across a page I'd folded over and wondered what was on it that I had wanted to remember. I found it two-thirds of the way down: *"People wish to be settled; only insofar as they are unsettled is there any hope for them."* Farther up, another thought catches my eye—on aging.

But the man and woman of seventy assume to know all, they have outlived their hope, they renounce aspiration . . . and talk down to the young. Let them become organs of the Holy Ghost, let them be lovers, let them behold truth, and their eyes are uplifted, their wrinkles smoothed, and they are perfumed again with hope and power. This old age ought not to creep on a human mind. In nature every moment is new; the past is always swallowed, the coming only is sacred.

☙

Rollo May writes [in *The Courage to Create*] of Prometheus's liver, how it restored itself at the beginning of each new day.

All artists have at some time had the experience at the end of the day of feeling tired, spent, and so certain they can never express their vision. . . . But during the night their liver grows back again. They arise full of energy and go back with renewed hope to their task, again to strive in the smithy of their soul."

☙

This morning I woke up wishing that Christmas could be just another day, that I didn't have to think about any part of it. When I went to Cross Brothers for ice cream, Norma was dressed in a red outfit with a ceramic Santa head on her sweater. "Dressed for Christmas," I said. "I'm trying," she said. I knew that if I scratched the surface I'd hear all about her money problems. This is the spirit or lack of it that my story [*Giovanni's Light*] deals with.

I must confess a shameful weakness, a failure to be consistently generous. After a brief period of time, I'm finished. I don't want to return to the bedside, the yard, or wherever it is that help is needed. I wonder if I fear becoming indispensable, that my first steps toward helping someone will trap me, make it difficult to leave. I wonder also if it is only if I hollow myself out in some way that involves prayer, even fasting, something I have never done in all my years on earth, that genuine generosity can emerge.

❦

I am so disappointed in myself. All these weeks of steadily losing weight are about to be undone. Is the reason for losing my way the belief that I cannot really do it? Well, I will not be a coward. I will confess, at least to myself, that I have fallen down, and I will get up again and continue with a hopeful heart. There are times when you must treat yourself like a child, with tenderness and belief and encouragement.

❦

A moment of quasi-enlightenment when I realized that I have been spending a lot of time in the past and it has had a demoralizing effect.

Recently I have been watching a lot of television and seeing many people I knew when I lived in Washington and worked for the *Post* and was on the *Newshour*. It made me aware of who I *used* to be, the friends and contacts I *used* to have. Then I thought how my phone *used* to ring a lot more, and how I *used* to be a lot busier. Revisiting my past had a paralyzing and narrowing effect on me. My capacity to be fully aware and connected to life as it is—instead of how it was—was diminished. Then, for a few liberating seconds, I got out from under the past and was free of it. Living in the past is the temptation and burden of aging.

I am also aware of a large inventory of experiences, of having been immersed in such beauty for all of my life. But even this can be a hindrance that creates a painful nostalgia for days gone by. The present becomes an empty antechamber where one sits thinking about what is on the other side of a locked door. It is also a temptation to view the present mournfully and worry that what we have will be taken away—as indeed it will.

For a moment I closed my eyes and imagined how it would be to let go of writing, to lose my grip on the chain of words that leads me through the darkness. Am I not a prisoner of words, dependent upon them in a way that tethers me to my own intellect? To always be looking down at a line of print instead of up at the world in front of me seems escapist. But I would no more remove myself from the page than I would take a rattle from a baby's hand. The ability to make my own noise is what makes me feel alive.

I broke down last night by the fire and told Mom I was really depressed. Almost too much to go into it. But I did, and she was so encouraging and convinced that all will be well. I read some excerpts from this journal to her. It seems to be the place I am writing best these days.

I am acutely aware that I am about to impoverish myself, to dig all the way into my meager stock portfolio, liquidate it, and pay bills that must be paid. Then comes my equity line, where I go back into debt, and then I am flat broke and gone. If I can get a few more students for my Ashland seminar, keep bringing in some mentoring fees, be very careful with my expenses, and perhaps count on Mother for $300 a month, we'll be okay.

Fear makes us take time-consuming detours around the thing we are afraid of. It is possible to live one's entire life this way, not going toward what we desire, avoiding what we cannot find the courage to confront. Every new apprehension is a new link in the chain of fears.

From a Merchant-Ivory screenplay I found in my office:

Her books about America no longer sell, and she is broke. This breaking up of a well-formed personality is what she is enduring now.

Exactly how I feel! Finding it in print cheered me up.

It is true that you become what you love. I love ideas, words, people, and food. So I am an intellectual with lots of friends who is twenty pounds overweight. If I were to love exercise, thrift, and truth I would be better off.

Watching Robin MacNeil on the *Newshour* last night as I rested on some folded laundry on my lap, I felt so helpless. What am I doing? I joked to my mother. I write the same chapter all day, don't go outside the house, and fold laundry. What I am missing is the feeling of being connected to the larger world. But this is something that can happen without physical movement. And I thought to myself that I should take the opportunity to connect with my interior world more deeply, even though it can feel murky and ill-defined.

How is it that I can go so long without being loved in a concrete physical way? [This is Catholic-girl speak for sex.] And have I lost the instinct for loving another in the same way? Writing it down makes me realize that it is a pretty insubstantial question/complaint. I am loved as much as I am able to receive it. That is the truth of it. And I do not feel that my capacity to receive love is very large. Again, it goes back to making room, allowing for it. What is present that should be removed in order to make it possible, self-loathing?

I am beginning, by small degrees, to realize how one might eventually become enlightened—not as the result of "heavy lifting" but by quietly reflecting, or coming upon an idea so integral that one is subtly, permanently, changed by it.

Another idea came to me last night as I was gathering my clothes and reading matter from the bathroom floor. My messy, demanding ego resists order, but my soul requires it. To quietly pick up after oneself is a soul-ordering activity that I have resisted most of my life. I'm not sure why. Being orderly is not that difficult. In fact, it is a very easy thing to do—if the ego can be trained to know its place.

It is consoling to think, if I am not always looking for God, that God is nevertheless looking for me. It is my suspicion, so deep that I forget its existence, that I am as profound as I am willing to be, that only a small revolution or turn toward the light would make all the difference.

2002

Yesterday was New Year's Day. I went to Cross Brothers Market and found a way to jump-start the book, give it life. It doesn't change anything so much as it makes the story open up, like a window, to let some air in. I owe it to Norma (renamed "grumpy Diane" in my book), who is always slipping terrible news into the conversation while she rings up my groceries. She was the Everywoman I needed to keep the story from being a fuzzy, Walt Disneyish reverie. Suddenly I was off, with my busybody character, Frances Nickerson, in hot pursuit. I continue to wonder if this is a children's story or whether it is an adult story with children in it. Dickens didn't make these distinctions.

Fear and facts are not the same thing, and when I think of my life I think I must treat the realities in it as facts, not fears. I am almost penniless. This is a fact. I am afraid of this fact. This is a fear. My book goes slowly. Fact. I am afraid of my book dying. Fear.

Yesterday I wrote a small three-page chapter, but it is complete. Chapter Four today.

I have been thinking of the whole concept of "losing heart." A squib in the *New York Times* reports that doctors now know that the heart can repair itself. Conversely, a heart can be destroyed by the possessor, and the emotional or psychological loss of heart is real, too.

My father's bad heart may have been made worse by the fact that he didn't believe in his own life, in its value, or in his capacity to survive his mistakes—his bad opinion of himself. This is enormously sad, and I wish I had known or felt able to approach him. But even if he were alive now, I don't think I would have the courage to approach him. He was too unbroken, like a horse that could kick you unawares.

I made the mistake of reading my book with fresh eyes, only to discover it wasn't what I thought it was—at least not yet. It took away the small platform of self-worth I had been standing on; immediately, everything ahead looked dark.

This morning I am feeling better. A pink shirt, a little moisturizer, and hair that falls correctly can have a restorative effect.

Reading, I come across the familiar phrase, "the story gripped him." Does *Giovanni's Light* grip me? Yes, it does. I am eager to get to the ending. Whether it is a children's story or not, I don't know, but it is a story with children in it.

Everything about yesterday restored me. I did nothing but make clay jugs and pots. In between, I took phone calls from friends and had a long satisfying talk with Christian [my older son]. Midday there was an unexpected gift of a box of L. L. Bean fatwood from the real Fran Nickerson. That night, Mom and I sat before the woodstove, swatting embers off our sweaters and the rug, while we fed the small aromatic sticks into the fire. A present like that, out of the blue and so exactly right from somebody so loved, is a plug for the wounded heart.

The chapter about Miranda Bridgeman is done. Somehow, despite the knowledge that I may be writing for a small family audience, I feel sure about the rightness of continuing. Five chapters done and now I'm at the sixth, where it is all new to me, except that it is the chapter where the town heads into darkness and starts to get sick—which may be too strong a word but accurate enough.

A letter from the real Fran Nickerson fighting for me, protesting against my self-doubt. Whenever I think of her, I see a crackling woodstove throwing off enormous heat. She inspires me to write—about her!

I find it interesting that writing fiction depends for me upon not knowing what I am going to say until I see it, while nonfiction is much more a distillation of ideas I have already written down. Yesterday, for instance, I wrote: *Edward Crimmins took his watch out of his vest pocket and laid it on the breakfast table*. Then, and only then, did I see what else—a stack of travel brochures—was also there. *Then he shook out his napkin*. You are only able to see where you are after you have arrived.

Another chapter written. I'm not sure of its quality. All one has to do is read a D. H. Lawrence story like "The Man Who Loved Islands," to know what seamless beauty is. Yet Lawrence lifts me up to a level I would forget if I wasn't standing on it—like a stair.

∽

Mom, on some of the people in Ashland:

"It's so sad. All they're doing is breathing. They have no vision of what their life is supposed to be for. They really truly feel that they don't have another life. This is it. When you die, you hope that you're saved. There's no sense that you incarnate. It's a dead end. You never get beyond the altar. The altar blocks them. I think if Jesus came back he would tear the altars down."

On one of her friends:

"There is something about me that brings out the second chakra [anger] in her. It just comes out of her. It's sad because there is so much inside her that doesn't come out. But she has chosen to lead the mundane life and be happy with it, and to tell herself that she's happy with it. She's going lickety-split around the wheel of life. It's depressing."

∽

I am reading a biography of Mark Twain in which the playwright Arthur Miller commented upon Twain's disastrous business sense. What Miller calls Twain's "excess of imagination" wrecked him and his family as he chased after wealth. Had he simply stayed at home and written, he would have been solvent throughout his life. This is a lesson I am learning right now—with almost no one signing up for Nightwriters and me in the hole at least $10,000 because of it.

∾

A conversation with a difficult friend. Talking to her is like going on a dangerous but exhilarating bobsled run. I'm always relieved to get off the sled intact.

∾

The snow chapter is almost done and Will has met Giovanni. Angels have been introduced, Miranda Bridgeman has been defined as a budding writer, which opens up some opportunities. It is a joy to have a few friends, like Pat and Mom, waiting in the living room each evening to hear the new installment. That and a block of clay to make little jugs and faces out of at the end of the day, and I'm provided for.

Lying in bed this morning, I became aware that I was in the midst of a battle for my spirit, or soul. And the battle is really with two selves, one that wants to imprison me and one that wants me to be free. All night long I let myself in and out of the same jail cell.

Then I think of my friend Sue, who is fighting it out on a literal level. After being in prison for fifteen years, she was recently paroled. She vacillates between fear and exhilaration. So much freedom, to make so many choices—and mistakes. When you are free you are unprotected from yourself.

Being a writer gives you the skeleton key to a lot of doors that wouldn't open otherwise. In 1994, I read a story in our local paper about Sue Kennon, a young woman inmate in a nearby Virginia penitentiary who was serving a forty-eight year sentence for multiple drug-related felonies. The mother of three small children, she was the first inmate to have gotten a college diploma while behind bars. I thought she sounded remarkable and wanted to become part of her support system. I wrote her a letter and she wrote back saying that the only way for us to meet was for me to give a writing seminar for the inmates, which I did—the first Nightwriters seminar behind bars.

For several months, I met once a week with a dozen women, most of them in prison for nonviolent crimes, like forging checks and drug prescriptions. Then the prison had a lockdown that kept all the women in their quarters, and the seminar came to an abrupt end. But through letters and visits, Sue and I maintained our friendship. During this time, she began work on her Masters in Psychology. Then, in 2001, she was unexpectedly paroled and now works for the state at that same prison, teaching women how to be parents behind bars.

I am on the chapter about Neddie and his father stuck in the house together in the blizzard. I'm not sure how to bring them together in an interesting way—something about time, and Neddie's father realizing that the snow has made time irrelevant—nobody can go anywhere so there's no need to know what time it is. This is the chapter where the town grinds to a halt and Edward Crimmins grinds to a halt, too. It is painful, but by the end of the day Neddie and his father are joined.

I am discovering the truth of the statement "Fiction is the highest form of history."

Dorothy, sitting upright on the sofa, listened to me read, and when I got to the part where Edward Crimmins starts to cry, she murmured, "He's been wantin' to cry all his life."

❦

I am taking a ceramics class in Richmond. It is difficult work, and the part of my personality that is seven years old and wants to cry with anger and frustration came leaping to the surface. That damn clay blob defeats me, turns into a mocking, rubber-lipped mouth. I resist wanting to know, in detail, how clay operates, how I must wedge the clay to get the molecular particles going in the same direction.

One of the more advanced students showed me her rubber "comb" and how you should push the clay gently to the side instead of tamping it down, as was my instinct. I was surprised at how respectful of the clay she was. She said she was like me when she started. I see how terribly impatient I am. Clay requires great patience or it won't respond.

❦

Last night when I came home from the dentist, Dorothy and Esther were waiting in the living room with Mother to hear the next installment in my story. What I like best about their reaction is that they can't tell what's going to happen next. I've discovered one possibly big flaw. Can Giovanni burn wet Christmas trees? The story depends upon his being able to do it.

It has been nagging at me that if this book is not accepted by a publisher I will be very, very depressed/angry/

helpless. But I must take that risk. I believe in this story and I will see it through.

It is difficult at this point in the story to do anything but write. I don't want to clean house, or take a walk, or pay attention to any other aspect of life. Like giving birth to a baby, it's stronger than any other impulse.

Now I am on Chapter Eleven, when it all comes together. My gentle listeners' response is still that no one knows what's going to happen until it happens, so that is a good sign. I don't know all the details myself until I get into the writing. The more I write, the more I see. It is an amazing process, and I see the connection between doing this in my life as well, taking steps forward, not knowing what to expect but going ahead anyway and then being able to perceive more.

Last night at a dinner party, I was aware of how the men there seemed to be locked into jails of different kinds. B was the biggest surprise. I thought he would be very charismatic and commanding; instead, he seemed worried and withdrawn. R was quiet for much of the time, like a judge listening to oral arguments, and K always seemed to be trying, via questions, to keep center stage. (The women, of course, were perfect.)

I finished Chapter Twelve—the final one—yesterday. My constant audience, Dorothy and Esther, were over promptly at five to hear it. They approved. "You leave the reader in another—better—place," is what Dorothy said. In talking to Justin on the phone and telling him I was really afraid of being disappointed (Would my agent like it? Would it sell?), he said, "You have to humble yourself and say that you love it. And that's all that matters. It's the work that is important." This morning I begin the rewrite. I must be careful not to ruin what is there.

Financially, I look a little better. Offers to edit, to help someone write a book; students for Nightwriters coming in, drip by drip. I am totally grateful to Mother, who has really been carrying the load.

∾

Up late last night clearing away papers and filing others, I discovered to my horror that I had overdrawn my never-empty Nightwriters account by paying the same bill twice. "Well," I said to myself, "you are responsible for this. What did you expect if you do not keep track?" Even my mother, half blind as she is, takes scrupulous care of her checkbook.

My writing seminars are failing, along with the economy after 9/11. This morning I will cancel Scotland and California but keep Italy or, more prudently, will not cancel Italy yet.

∾

Mother's life continues to amaze me. For the past several months during her meditations, she has seen an endless succession of intricate three-dimensional geometric shapes, moving slowly in front of her closed eyes, often with shapes behind shapes, transparent and without color. These "building blocks of the universe," as she calls them, are as clear to her as if she were looking at them in a book. So, too, are the spirit people she sees—most recently in Ukrop's Market—who are also transparent and move down the aisles in such numbers toward her that she has to stop and ground herself by looking at her feet. Then, when she looks up again, they have thinned out or are gone.

I have asked Mom whether she can see their faces clearly. She said yes. Are they agitated? No, just serious. Headed for her specifically? Some are, some aren't. Is she frightened? Not at all. What does it mean? She doesn't know but if she is meant to help them she doesn't feel inclined to do it. She is more interested in tracking down the geometric designs, finding out how and what she is supposed to do with them; clearly, she said, these are gifts given to her after her eyesight began to go. The color purple came first, then the spirit people, which she would just as soon do without, and now these beautiful designs and shapes.

One evening we talked at length about how it is to go blind. "There are compensations if you allow them," she said. "If you resist, there aren't any." She sleeps better because her mind is emptier. She sees things whole, even though she cannot see them completely. "Like the Wehman's tulips. I become one with them, swim in the color; I'm suffused with it." So, too, was she. (The irony was that she was getting more beautiful as she was less able to see herself in the mirror.) "Life is simpler," she continued. "I'm living a larger existence in a smaller, more circumscribed space." She was not looking at me as she spoke. The habit of looking me in the eye was leaving her.

I am sitting with a second draft of *Giovanni's Light* on my lap. Yesterday it went off to Molly [my agent]. I am pleased with it. Little bits of writing gleam on the page in a way that makes me happy, and I think the characters are real. I feel like all of them in some way.

❧

This morning, on my birthday, I gave a friend with the same birthday a present of some inspirational quotations in a box. Before I left, I urged him to pick one and read it. He chose one by Eleanor Roosevelt: "Always do what you are afraid to do." Well, I thought, I have to call Molly and find out what she thinks of my book.

To know by the end of the day whether my book is considered good enough by Molly for presentation requires a detachment that is not natural to me. Yet I am steadier than the circumstances would warrant. My mind, or spirit, feels vigorous and hopeful, as if, on some deeper level, all is resolved.

❧

Last night, I replayed for the hundredth time what Molly told me when I called. It is "utterly, utterly wonderful," she said. "It reads itself; what's not to love?" In other words, Molly was blown away by it and agrees with me that it's a book with children in it *and* a children's book. "A classic crossover book," she said. I can hardly believe the words. It put me in an entirely new reality, one that frankly I had not imagined—to hear Molly be so transported. She had been stressed out and tired when she got on the train Thursday night in New York. She had 1,400 pages of manuscripts to read and decided to read the least number of pages first—which meant mine. And by the time she was done, she had calmed down, felt in an entirely new place, and went to bed early. The book had acted as a tranquilizer, she said. If Molly likes it, the book will get sold but I must not think that it will be a great financial boon. What I do hope for it is that it will be read.

It is amazing to think that a month ago I was broke and yesterday I bought material to slipcover two living room chairs.

❧

The town has suffered another tragedy. A man in a small house on North James Street was beaten to death. Scratch the surface and this town seeps with tales. I find it interesting that Ashland seems to be more transparent than usual, the stories coming fast and furious through the door. Murders, betrayals, bankruptcies, PTA mothers getting arrested, blood pressures rising or sinking with news. Mother comes home from her walks with new stories every day—and I make note of them.

A call from Molly, who has shopped my book around. Virginia Duncan (from Greenwillow) does not like it. Nan Graham (at Scribner's) does, with more work. We shall see. Molly speaks of adding about thirty pages, which expands it by a third. I cannot imagine at this moment where or how to do it but am willing to try. I think the key is to look more closely at everything. My present instinct is to stick with my vision of it being a book for children that adults would read. It will take time for Molly to pull this off. I must simply wait.

❧

Today, the Immaculate Degenerates had Tommy Willis, the owner of Cross Brothers Market, talk to them about the history of his store. I took notes:

Once, Tommy delivered groceries to a woman who lowered a bucket from the second floor of her house.

Then there was the woman who came by at closing time wanting a cooked chicken. They had one left in the meat locker. He brought it out. The woman asked if he had a larger one. Tommy took it back and returned with the same chicken. "I believe I'll take both of them," she said. Not to be outwitted, Tommy said he couldn't do that; he had promised to take one home to his wife for supper.

He told the tale of the man who dropped off a whole truckload of cardboard boxes behind the store. Tommy got so mad he loaded them into his truck and drove to the man's house late at night and dumped them back on his front lawn. Then he stayed up all night feeling guilty. I'm just as big an SOB as he is, he thought, and before dawn he drove back to the man's house, loaded all the boxes back onto his truck, and took them back to the store. Later, his wife told him that she had given the man permission to use their trash container.

He recalled a comment from Mrs. Newton Priddy, who would call in her orders. "Get me some of that number twenty-five flour, but don't sell me no bag the damn cat sat on."

Tommy Willis was one of the first people I got to know when I moved to Ashland. In his sixties, with wavy silver-gray hair (more on that in a minute) and a dry sense of humor, he is usually cleaning out the onion bin or stocking canned goods and is ready to talk—which is one of my requirements for friendship—when I come into the store. Over the years, Tommy has told me about his men's singing group (which goes on fun road trips), his antique car collection, and how his wife, a retired hairdresser, sets his hair with marcel clips every morning after breakfast and puts him under a hair dryer while he reads the newspaper. I love to think about that.

Several years ago, Tommy invited me to an ice cream social at his church, which was just winding up its annual revival week. I had never been to an ice cream social or a revival, and the idea of going to the Hopeful Baptist Church with Tommy's family seemed like a unique out-of-time way to spend the afternoon. The following Sunday I found myself sitting in a small country church, full of men in double-breasted suits and women with bertha collars, singing "What a Friend We Have in Jesus." As the late afternoon sun filled the church up with honey-colored light, I felt as if I were in a National Geographic article about the American heartland.

Then came the ice cream social in the basement. Tommy stood with me in line and whispered, "See that lady up ahead, with her husband?" I followed his gaze to a gray-haired woman with glasses, wearing a pleated skirt and a sweater set. She looked like all the other parishioners at Hopeful Baptist—old-fashioned and decent, with kitchen drawers full of neatly folded Clorox-scented dish towels. Her husband, dropping scoops of ice cream on her plate, wore a Mr. Rogers zip-up cardigan sweater over his shirt and tie.

"What about them?"

"She found him on line," he whispered. "In Florida."

"You're kidding! You mean they're newlyweds?"

Tommy nodded. "But you can bet she had him checked out six ways to Sunday before she got involved."

I would have reason to think back to this conversation later on.

❦

Up early, my one cup of coffee already consumed. My thoughts race ahead of the light. Today is the day Molly negotiates a deal with Scribner's. Nan will, I think, bid on my book. Molly will, I know, represent me well. And it remains for me to reinforce the themes that want strengthening. I see it as a joy and am so relieved that Nan does not want a wholesale revision, which I could not do. I am already planning to turn the garage into a guest cottage to bring in extra income.

Around noon, Molly called me to say she had talked to Nan. "You can buy one cashmere sweater," she said. Then, without further ado, she dropped the news: seventy-five thousand dollars! In my wildest fantasies I had not allowed myself to think of an amount this high. Mother broke into tears when I told her. After living so close to the bone, with so little margin for error, it seems like a staggering amount of money.

I am reminded of the time I stood behind Nora Ephron in the elevator of her apartment building in New York, watching her rip open her mail and pull out checks as casually as little Valentines, barely reading the amounts. Money seems to be pouring in again, but the instinct to save is neither strong nor weak. On some level, money itself just doesn't catch my attention, except when the lights go out.

❦

I find it interesting that I know Mother so well I can predict what she is going to want almost every minute of the day: the cup of coffee, the cigarette, the glass of port by the fire. She is, on the one hand, so materially bound, on the other, so spiritually free.

A long satisfying conversation with Eliza. There is no one I would rather have as a daughter—and she made me laugh when she said she had been headed toward another mother but hung a right at the last moment and wound up with me. [My two oldest children are adopted.]

I am so moved by David McCullough's biography of John Adams, who inspires one to be virtuous and openhearted, without guile or malice. McCullough quotes a letter from Adams to a grandchild:

Do justly love mercy. Walk humbly. This is enough. . . . So questions and so answers your affectionate grandfather.

And another:

He who loves the Workman and his work and does what he can to preserve and improve it, shall be accepted of Him.

After a weekend of gardening and cleaning out the garage, it now stands ready to be renovated. The pleasure I get back from this house on this piece of land is continual. There is a certain moment in the late afternoon when the sun slips out from behind a cloud, like a monstrance raised to catch the light—and light floods the air, intensifies and suffuses everything, and then quickly recedes. Every living thing thrums and glows, and the amazing fact is that no one sitting quietly on the porch chatting about whatever we are discussing ever pauses to remark on the beauty that surrounds us.

Lately I have been sitting for a few minutes after my morning walk, on the bench at the edge of the park pond. At this time of year, with the trees in new bud, their leaves hang like small pale flags from the branches and a light mist of pollen covers the pond. A pair of mallards have taken up residence at the south end. Usually one is resting on the bank while the other swims. What particularly impresses me is the way one can interpret and then reinterpret the same scene.

Last night, watching a beautifully done documentary on the mollusk, whose most brilliant relative is the chambered nautilus, I was struck by the truly magnificent, inspired nature of creation, the way the nautilus traps gas in its separate chambers so it can float. Then I get a tooth removed and am told that after the blood clot gives way to new nerves, the nerves will proceed to rebuild the bone. The cells know!

A week from now I will be in California, waking up in Francesca's guest room, listening to the Pacific Ocean a block away. This is an amazing fact that never gets less so. But more amazing is the realization that, no matter where I am, I have come together as a whole person in a way I never thought possible. Those years of longing for another have come to an end, or at least a surcease. That being said, I wonder how this will change when Mother moves on.

An overcast, cool morning. Sitting by De Jarnette Pond. Both ducks were on the grass where they had been before, the male mallard on both feet, with his neck fully extended upward, the female with one leg tucked up and her neck sunk in an S upon her chest. I wondered what they had to protect them against predators, and then, of course, I remembered: wings. The equivalent in humans is the imagination.

A silent flotilla of leaves, too light to sink, drifts slowly with the wind across the surface of the pond. On the ground, there are more of those little one-wing propeller-shaped seeds, so easy to ignore unless you're looking—like the pair of gray upside-down squirrels clinging to the gray tree trunk. Nature usually clothes its creatures so modestly.

Mother announced yesterday that her "French leg" (the one that was mangled by the Dalmatian dog that ran into her in Menton on the Riviera) was giving her the same pain walking that it did two years ago, before she began taking glucosamine and chondroitin. "Oh, well, the end of an era (i.e., walking)," she said. "It's something to build on." I know her well enough to know that not walking is a deeply disappointing thought, that she is, on one level, very upset. On another level, she isn't.

This is the true joy in life, the being used for a purpose recognized by yourself as a mighty one; the being thoroughly worn out before you are thrown on the scrap heap; being a force of nature instead of a feverish selfish little clod of ailments and grievances complaining that the world will not devote itself to making you happy.
—George Bernard Shaw, *Man and Superman*

It is a mild, faintly muggy morning. The air is just moist enough to carry the scent of flowers on it like a handkerchief. The magnolia will open soon. The pond at De Jarnette Park smells of new rainwater. And our newly ousted mayor of Ashland is spitting mad! We have a brand-new town council that has never looked so diverse: two women, two black men, one white man.

∽

Most important occurrence of the day: Nan Graham's note, which arrived on Saturday.

Dear Phyllie,
Thank you. It's a thing of beauty. . . . *Giovanni's Light* has gone into production and will be in the stores for Christmas.

I called Molly and read her Nan's note. After all the Sturm und Drang she generated during our editing, Nan's sunny side is a relief.

Having written a work of fiction, I am finding my consciousness greatly expanded, as if my "closet" now has a wardrobe full of clothes for all kinds of people, not just for me.

Walking back from downtown yesterday, I took the top off a garbage can and tossed my newspaper into it. Suddenly a story began to take form in my mind. There was a discarded baby in the can and the casual act of discarding a newspaper saved the baby from dying of hypothermia. I played with that idea all the way home.

∽

Lunch with my friends Lee and Carol. The conversation turned to religion and what each of us believed. I found myself saying that I was much more conscious of light than darkness and I didn't really hold out much hope for myself changing. Lee said that not believing in sin didn't make sense and I agreed—but it was the guilt-inducing aspect of Christianity that felt so wrong.

Later, while talking with Mother and a neighbor, Sandy, I asked Mother who she thought God was. She answered that God was light. "And what do you do with it?" Sandy asked. "Nothing," said Mother. "I just allow it to bring me and my surroundings into greater harmony."

Searching for a way to say a few words about my mother's spiritual beliefs, I opened up a journal I kept specifically to record some of our conversations. Tucked in front was a letter she had written to me in her seventies, when she was in France.

Am sitting outside reading Emerson. I am completely, finally, enthralled with his writing. Where have I been?

Let me try to answer that.

In her midfifties, when she was still married to my father, my mother met Dr. Lawrence McCafferty, a spiritual teacher of metaphysics who had a profound impact upon the rest of her life. Lawrence, as his disciples called him, opened the door to a world that, intuitively, my mother already knew existed. He taught her how to experience it—through a series of public discourses, private sessions, use of Tarot cards, and most especially meditation. He died in 1979, about ten years after she met him, and long before she came to live with me, but many of his talks had been recorded. At my house, my mother had an entire library of his tapes beneath her bed.

Every morning, while I sat in the living room reading, writing, and free-form floating around in my mind, my mother was in her room, listening to a tape, meditating, or doing her yoga exercises—usually in that order. The rest of the day was spent waiting to see what it might bring forth—a walk, a visit from a friend followed by a phone call from one of her children, or a trip to the library for another Maeve Binchy novel on tape (she was addicted to them). But running quietly beneath the surface of her life, what she was really doing was waiting, as patiently as she could, for her own death.

"When you leave this plane," she once said, "the postmortem life isn't that different because you bring your consciousness with you. In fact, that's all you bring. Most people don't know that."

One night, when her eyes were still good enough to play cards, I decided to give her a small tutorial on the computer. Sitting her down in front of the keyboard, I showed her how she could play Solitaire on the screen.

She wasn't impressed. "I like to hold the cards in my hand," she protested.

I decided to introduce her to Google. "You can look up anything," I said.

"Really?"

"Yes, just give me something to search for."

"Could you look up the Akashic Records?"

"The what?" I had never heard of them. But after I typed it into the search box, up came the Wikipedia definition: "Sanskrit for a compendium of mystical knowledge encoded in a non-physical plane of existence."

When my mother was a little girl, she used to spend long lonely hours staring into the pond behind her house, wishing she had the courage to dive in and join the Water Babies who swam around the bottom. That same innocence and inclination of heart stayed with her to the end. She believed in Everything and the Akashic Records is where Everything can be found.

I wonder how much of the clear-mindedness, peace, and comfort I feel now is related to the absence of daily worry and responsibility for my children. The fear that laced my life, needing to know they were alive and well, was constant. Waking up from a nap always meant asking myself, "Where are they?" Now, however, I do not want to push myself into any new zones of discomfort or pain of that kind.

Yesterday, standing in a supermarket line, I read aloud a Mary Oliver poem to Mother and realized what a sharp knife to the soul she is. Instantly, I moved to a richer, deeper place in my consciousness. But generally I have noticed that I am very easily distracted when I am reading. My capacity to be at one with the words I am trying to digest is weak. Remembering what I have read is harder.

Almost everything I do is done in a preoccupied state, and only writing, which requires attention to the pen, the paper, and the line of thought across the page, has the capacity to focus my attention. If I could really see how this habit of mind hinders me, I wouldn't have so many exploding eggs in the pot on the stove.

The mind, I am convinced, is its own apothecary, dumping chemicals into our bloodstream that go to the brain and influence the thoughts we have and the impressions we receive. And the mind knows what to avoid that might bring us pain.

Last night, for example, I placed my new digital camera on my desk and posed in front of it. I could not affect a single flattering pose. The face I possess was just not the face I thought was mine and I am amazed at the disparity. Later, when I stood in front of a mirror and stared quietly at my reflection, I was brought up-to-date again. This is not a face that would turn anyone's head. I could not even find clues of distinctiveness or elegance. It was simply a lump, intelligent but not beautiful.

Mom's eighty-fifth birthday. My present to her is to be at her disposal for the entire day. She is such a continual gift, when I imagine her gone I cannot quite see myself here. Yet she has brought such peace to my life that I cannot imagine that peace leaving when she dies.

It was a day of family phone calls, flowers, a drop-in from Mel and the boys, crab cakes with Pat, and small acts of love from me—a new cotton blanket for her bed, another book tape (*Les Miserables*)—and then it was over.

After dinner on a dark porch, we talked quietly about her last "seven-year cycle" and how joyful and complete it had been. Two estranged children speaking to her again, the blessings that came after the deterioration of her eyes—"and living with you," she said, "is one of them." If she completes another cycle she will be ninety-two, which seems unlikely. But I hope she will be here long enough for me to finish the book about her.

Summer has come and the heat has released the perfume from the earth. As I ride my bicycle through the street, my nose is filled with the scent of the flowers and grasses that are at the height of their lushness. All the magnolias are in bloom. I dip my nose into the cup of their petals and can't believe my luck. De Jarnette Pond, swirling with arabesques of algae, is new every morning.

Mother didn't feel well yesterday. I stayed close and made an effort to do things for her—vacuuming her room, arranging her books, etcetera. Late last night I massaged her back and feet, trying to run strength into her body through my hands. This morning she pronounced herself cured, saying that my hands had healed her. I do think about what life will be like when she is gone, but it seems impractical to advance the plot. Right now is where I am.

Sometimes it is so quiet here in Ashland that I wonder how we don't die of it. There is nothing to remind you from the outside that you are here. I understand why it is so hard to get people to visit. They know what they will find, a quietness so deep and steady it creates a kind of nervousness. I visualize Eudora Welty in Jackson, Mississippi, the lace curtains in her living room catching the lemon-colored light every afternoon, even the dust undisturbed on the floor. One must have a very active imagination to withstand it.

It occurs to me that I am going backward, into the same but different state of life I chafed to leave when I was young. Too quiet, too spare, too beyond my ability to make exciting. Yet my childhood was the real time of richness from which I continue to draw my creativity. So here I am again, a child of quiet.

❧

A conversation with the wife of a former college president. She said that her husband had gone into a deep depression just before he retired and that five years later he was not yet out of it. "He's busy," she said, "but that's all it is." There is a growing segment of the population that is silently suffering from lack of meaning. The little sand castles of accomplishment begin to crumble before their eyes, and the question of what life is for, returns to be answered.

Last night at the library I saw a neighbor whom I hadn't seen for over a year. The miracle was remembering his name. With so much forgetting that is going on, it's thrilling to do a little remembering. The mind is like a library full of overloaded shelves. As you age, the shelves collapse and one is forced to throw things into a pile that hides what lies in it. This is the best metaphor I can think of.

❧

From *Henry Miller on Writing*:

What happened to me in writing . . . was tantamount to revelation. It was revealed to me that I could say what I wanted to say—if I thought of nothing else, if I concentrated upon that exclusively—and if I were willing to bear the consequences which a pure act always involves.

Yesterday, I spent the afternoon on the James River with my friends the Roepers. The James revealed no secrets, but the deep quiet pools and little rushing waterfalls, safe enough for children, were beautiful and green. A blue heron unfolded its wings and flapped across the water. A large crowd of geese slid like a moving carpet above the bow of our boat, and nets of mosquitoes, almost invisible, hovered just over the water, moving as one. Sitting in the boat, tightly cinched into a life vest and helmet, with clunky tennis shoes and wet clothing, I felt as ungainly as a wet sandbag. Trying to climb rocks near the shore in rubber sneakers was impossible. Twice I slipped back into the water when my shoes lost their grip.

Today was spent scrubbing and hosing down the side porch. Then in the later afternoon I discovered Eckhart Tolle in *Sun* magazine. Many of his ideas about time and living in the present mirror mine. Only children live in the present; only people with time on their hands see clearly. Thinking about how Ashland has changed me, it was here that my first prolonged period of daily ecstasy as an adult took place. I would wake up and smell the air flowing over my windowsill and notice the way the light caught the smallest hairs around a lilac leaf.

Late yesterday afternoon, I sat alone on the back porch, listening to the soft buzz of insects in the warm air. My imagination traveled back to California when I was a teenage girl with all my life before me. The amber quiet, the smell of dry leaves and water, and the sharp particularity that was so much a part of that time when I automatically noticed everything—the grooves in the porch railing, the hairs of my own arm—are with me again.

Nikki Hardin said last night on the phone that she felt invisible. Children feel that, too, but it seems like the natural state of things to a child. Then, once you lose the color and vividness of youth, you are invisible again. But it does give one the power to observe life without being seen, like a ghost.

I spent time with an elderly friend of mine today. Her story, of being a World War II bride and then rising with her husband's career, is so typical, and why shouldn't it be? Every story is typical. We just don't see it that way because we cannot rise one millimeter above the wave of events in which we are trapped, like a strand of seaweed, traveling alongside millions of other strands of seaweed, toward the same shore.

Last night, sitting on my neighbor Dolo Kerr's front porch, on her swing, was a wonderful way to end the day. Katherine Tinker came over for a while, to say that her dog, Jacob Morley, is dying. Then the town police pulled up in front of the apartment on the other side of the tracks. Dolo said this is frequent. There have been drug dealers and prostitutes living there. Meanwhile, we swing back and forth in the moonlight. The wisteria grabs the white wooden porch columns for support, the cat Lucy scratches the screen door, wanting to get outside. It's not New York, although twice while we were talking a train that takes you to New York rolled by.

I took an evening walk. The moon was up and the town took on a different, more solemn dimension, as if the night colors made it more solitary and mysterious. The smoker was on his corner, neatly dressed in black pants and a white short-sleeved shirt, the fingers of his right hand shoved into his pocket as they always are, the elbow of his left arm close to his side, like a towel rack that comes out from the waist and angles up, his fingers delicately pinching the end of his cigarette. I had given him a wife who wouldn't let him smoke in the house, but I'm told that he lives alone and does nothing but read. The smoker is a slight man, perhaps 145 pounds, with pale pink skin and white hair. He seems alert but dreamy, his eyes fixed at some point straight ahead that is across the street from where he stands.

On Saturday I spent quite a lot of time making things Mom wants to do possible. We went to the nursery and bought Katherine Tinker a pussy willow plant in memory of Jacob Morley, who had just died. After delivering it, the three of us spent the rest of the morning in Katherine's tree house eating watermelon. Then, late at night before bedtime, we sat on our porch and I read to Mother from Hugh I'Anson Fausset's autobiography, *A Modern Prelude*. Finally, holding an oil lamp in one hand to light the page, I read sonnets from an anthology of poetry. Mother didn't know what a sonnet was and asked me if I had learned about them in school. As I was reading to her and explaining certain things, like the iambic pentameter rhyme scheme and the sonnet form, I felt my good fortune to be the one chosen to make her ready for the end of her earthly life. It is transforming *me* to be the one who is with her. The beauty of it came over me as I sat there and read from Shakespeare and Milton and Edna St. Vincent Millay. We ended with Milton's "On His Blindness."

For several hours on Sunday I sorted through old letters, dating back to 1985, keeping only those written to or from family. It was not a pleasant experience, and by the end of it I wondered whether it wasn't, at base, unnatural. So much pain and darkness hovered over the pile. The past is material for the present, but if we save it to justify ourselves or hurt others we weigh the present down. The past kills. Memories make wars, and a letter to or from an ex-spouse is a sharp knife, capable of inflicting great damage—upon one's innocent children or oneself.

After it was done and I hauled large garbage bags full of letters downstairs, I couldn't help but think about the way the rest of nature vanishes without a trace when it is finished. Trees, snails, rivers—nothing leaves a record for its own sake. Everything dissolves back into the earth for future use, except humans.

Was there anything worth saving? I don't know, other than a few *New Yorker* jokes and newspaper photos that might be interesting later on. I was mildly surprised to realize how frequently my agent, Molly, wrote to me, and once, rather sternly, about my complaints about money. All in all, I felt as if I'd been walking across a killing field, and couldn't get the stench out of my clothes.

Is there a good reason to save my own letters as well as others? What, except a disinterested posterity, are they for? To know how one lived? I found that my cancelled checks from the 1970s came closer to the unwarped truth.

∽

Yesterday, I became a cell phone user. Again. This one can give callers my global position and collect my e-mail. It relieves Mother and estranges me. So much of my life is now online. Yesterday also marks the day I signed a contract with a local builder to remodel my garage.

∽

NOTES AFTER TRAVELING TO NEW YORK TO DO RESEARCH FOR THE BOOK ABOUT MY MOTHER

One should never go too long without taking a trip. The eye and sensibilities need the shake-up, even if it is not pleasant, and there were moments in this trip that I felt very real and uncomfortable emotions, the kind I experienced as a growing child, with the same lack of context or perspective that makes feelings so difficult to bear.

The impression I had of Mother's birthplace in East Islip was twofold: beautiful and boring. The bright simplicity of the marshes and the bay, combined with the empty lives of her family and the mindless shooting at birds from duck blinds, canceled each other out.

∽

A conversation with Mother:

MOTHER: The word *journaling*. Everybody's saying that. Are you?

Me: No way.

Mother: Would you say that *journaling* is a new idiom?

Me: No, it's a new word. An idiom is an expression, like *no way*."

Mother: Thank you. I must learn these things before I go on.

❧

Jon Longaker's funeral yesterday. There was a full church with all of Ashland in attendance. John McDowell's sermon was his usual, enthusiastic, slightly tangled message, but he had cut short his vacation to be there. He was tremendously consoling to Jon's widow, Lyde, and is by all accounts a kind and comforting pastor, so the church has flourished under his care.

Church is like Noah's Ark. They come in pairs and sit in the pews like they're glued to each other. The price for being free—to come and go as I please—is to feel slightly unpopular in this setting. But my pleasure comes from enjoying the faces as they take their places in the pews and march back from communion. Like speed-reading a lot of books. It catches me up on the town.

The quieter cycles of life are what fill me. The Reihl's garden is finally exhausted, leaving only the crepe myrtles to pick. But at last, Conde Hopkins's popcorn hydrangea bush has begun to bloom, and that will carry me over for at least two weeks. This house is very flower-dependent. What I love about Ashland is the abundance of them.

This morning I am reading from Robert Ellsberg's *The Saints' Guide to Happiness* and it reminds me of the real road I am on, where, as Dag Hammarskjold wrote, one should not seek death "but seek the road which makes death a fulfillment."

Yesterday, Mother said she had something to say to me. "Come into my room and sit down." (For such a soft-spoken person, she can be quite dramatic.) "I woke up this morning," she said, "and realized that I had already lived this day, so I don't have to live it again. I don't want to have any responsibilities, answer any phones, or see any people."

"So you want to go on a retreat?" I asked.

"It's more than a retreat," she answered, but she didn't elaborate.

All day, she stayed quietly in her room. I respected her wishes and did not intrude. Then, around five o'clock, she emerged. As we sat on the screened porch with our drinks, I asked her how it had been. "I was in space," she said, "and my mind was still the whole time. I could hear the birds and squirrels and I was present throughout, but even my body was silent." For someone I see every day, she is always interesting.

A few days later, Mother told me somewhat sheepishly that she had thought it was going to be the day of her death and she had wanted to be prepared.

On the subject of death, my mother was both practical and eager. A notarized DO NOT RESUSCITATE order hung on the inside of her closet door. Her POWER OF ATTORNEY form was right behind it. And when a volunteer from the local rescue squad came around looking for a donation, she wanted to be assured that they car-

ried morphine on their trucks before she wrote them out a check. Frequently, she began a sentence with "When I drop the old body . . ." or "After I'm gone . . . ," the latter usually tacked on to a request to make sure I put a towel down on the drainboard when I do the dishes or a reminder to get the screens replaced before they get any more ripped up.

Most afternoons, she and Dorothy Jones took their walk in the local cemetery, which Mother realized was slightly bizarre. They were two old ladies staggering around a bunch of tombstones "like phantoms in drag," she joked. But it didn't faze her. "Wherever you go you've got the soil for the new if you want it," she said. "Like the cemetery. If you put yourself right in it, you get to love it. The cemetery keeps you very aware of the present. You realize we're all headed there. It's just part of the game plan."

Game plan or not, I didn't like the idea of her not being downstairs when I was upstairs. She knew it and one evening, while we were having our usual drink before dinner, the subject turned to what it would be like for me after she died. "You may not believe this, but after I'm gone I'll be even closer to you than I am now. All the barriers will be dissolved."

I knew what she meant but could not bear to take the conversation any further.

Visiting the Artiglias yesterday afternoon, I was immersed in little boys and tree frogs, cicadas, June bugs, and developing tadpoles caught in the Witt's pond. Cody has brought back some algae tablets from the pet store; there is much searching for the dechlorinating drops. Everything in the house is about nature and the boys' love and fascination with it. The house is topsy-turvy, but one feels very much at home there.

Watering the plants yesterday afternoon, I was amazed to see how a spiderweb strung between a bush to the roofline survived the continued blast from my hose. The water simply blew through it, leaving the web unimpaired. How could this be?

A call from a young friend who is struggling hard to find meaning in the breakup with her boyfriend. She asked me to pray for her and him. Always she includes him. She goes over how he phrased things, looking for hope. "He wouldn't have said he wanted a separation if he really wanted to break up forever." I felt duty-bound to say that in my experience men can be cowards. I wanted to tell her that she is young and will feel happy again, but you can't jerk someone into the sunlight when grief is all they have left. We can see nothing with grief-struck eyes. This is what *blind with grief* means. *Blind with love* is the companion condition, when we see things that may not really be there either.

The question could be asked: "How much of my life is now lived in the present?" Without having a precise way to measure, I would answer, "More." More than when I had children around me and lovers to long for and was so pulled around by fear and desire. Now my life no longer revolves around things I cannot control.

The long summer drought is a good metaphor for the value of putting down deep roots. The trees remain green for that reason. But the grasses have turned to toast. Finally, last night, after weeks of no rain, it came. This morning the streets are steaming with mist and the smell of moist earth.

∾

A twenty-four hour trip to Washington cheered my heart. The physical look of the capital, the lineaments of its "face," are dear to me, like the actual faces of the friends I saw when I was there. I never wonder if my friends are looking forward with as much eagerness to seeing me. If I were to stop and ask, I would say no, that the larger pleasure is always mine.

I am up extremely early—three-thirty or four— and Mother is in her room listening to Lawrence (on tape). Sometimes when I think about writing about her, I feel over-whelmed. The mother of the present is so rich that I do not want to do the introductions. Perhaps I should begin in the present and then drop back.

Yesterday, before I left for Washington, I was in the kitchen and Mom was there, fussing about whether I had water to drink in the car, and so on. And then, out of the blue, she put her arms around me and said how much she loved me, how much she loved my spirit. It was very moving, and I drove up to Washington feeling cherished and warm.

Reading Etty Hillesum's diary [*An Interrupted Life*] is like returning to the heart of the matter. Only time, which is noth-ing, separates her from me. When I look at the photographs of her friends and marvel at the beauty and sensitivity in their faces, I feel as if I know them, which is how I feel generally about people. Standing on a street corner can feel like a class reunion.

Eckhart Tolle's *The Power of Now* is enlightening, and enlightenment is his topic. I am creeping up on the meaning of that word and feel that it has a connection to the way one was as a child, in a state of continual reception, without judgment, only wonder. Perhaps this explains my desire, which is increasing, to sit and *not* write in my journal but simply to be. Yet turning off the thinking mind remains elusive. I am still on the horse, wandering around, glued to the saddle.

It is important to set down on paper—so one can really look at them—what one's deepest desires in life are. I continue to return to the desire for a large and loving heart. I would like that most of all. Then I desire to be more disciplined and fruitful.

The first day of school after the summer: order, cool air, yellow school buses, children lined up for the new year of classes. All across the country the business of life resumes and I am calmed by it, given a sense of direction that it is summer's purpose to dissolve. Soon there will be fires in the living room and color in the trees.

My younger brother Peter flew from California to visit Mom for the first time since she moved here. She knew why he had come, to make sure he didn't miss the chance to be with her before she

*died. My youngest brother, Tony, was scheduled to come later.
"So, Peter, do you have any questions about me or your life that
you want me to try to answer?" "No, Mom," he said. "We're
square."*

Peter's visit has been all I had hoped it would be, and the surprise was his avid curiosity and delight in everything he saw
and read. He devoured a book of Jefferson's letters in a single
night, stayed up to read the manuscript of *Giovanni's Light,* and
has gone through photo albums with Mother, asking questions.
His way of thinking and expressing himself delights me.

Peter's last words as we drove him to the airport
were, "You're just what a big sister should be. You've got
things under control."There was not a single hitch in his visit
all week, and the events seemed perfectly orchestrated, ending with the BurntTaters at the coffeehouse last night. Before
that, we had dinner with the Browns, Lemons, Artiglias, and
others. It was a warm finish to a warm week and the mystery
of Peter's beginnings—as the solemn unsmiling child who
didn't think clowns were funny—is even deeper, given the
sunny open-hearted person he is now.

Fully alive. To be honest, open, and detached. This last is difficult. When I am angry, whatever pretensions to maturity
I have are shredded. When I am ignored, it hurts my vanity.
There are aspects of aging that no one is prepared for—and
being marginalized is a significant one. No wonder old men
father babies to keep themselves in the midst of things. Unless
you are able to let go, to reinvent yourself and endure the pain
of feeling your ego collapse around the truth, which is always

changing, getting older is not a gift. But we had better make it one or be left with the knowledge that we have been ungrateful for life itself.

ON THE PAIN OF LOSING A FRIEND THROUGH MISHANDLING

I think it is so difficult to lose a friend because there is a side of ourselves that is forever hidden except in their specific presence. We miss them, in part, because we miss that part of ourselves that is only activated in their presence. Conversely, there are people we avoid because they bring out parts of ourselves we would prefer not to look at. The sad thing is that when friends withdraw from us it is often because we bring out the worst in them.

A quick trip to New York made me long to be there more. When I emerge from Penn Station into the soupy air that smells of grime and chestnuts, old urine and sun, I feel connected to the world again. Everybody I brush by gives me energy, so that by the time I am halfway down the block I feel huge with life, even if I have no one to meet.

Subways are particularly evocative. I watched a young couple standing by the doors, swaying gently toward each other, so filled with attraction I marveled at their ability to keep their clothes on. Aboveground, there is such brilliant packaging of goods. A two-block stretch of Columbus Avenue easily relieved me of a hundred dollars: magazines, a shirt, a cup of coffee, and several bottles of olive oil and balsamic vinegar from a tiny, perfectly appointed shop that sold nothing but Italian oil, vinegar, salt, olives, and dipping dishes. Next door was a shop that sold nothing but products containing lavender.

Without a place to land, except a Starbucks, and having to drag a suitcase behind, one feels semihomeless. But what a rich human feast it is! My mind is restrung, my senses are more alert, and I think of Thomas Merton's line about "everyone walking around shining like the sun."

The joy to me was being with my friends Robert Ellsberg and Molly Friedrich for a few uninterrupted hours, talking about books and ideas and people while never running out of enthusiasm. Both of them are so alive, with a kind of wholeness and humor that pours out of them.

Molly's house in Bedford Hills is perfect: a rambling yellow empire with places in and around it where children can develop, like negatives, in their own time. I loved the dogwood at the top of the hill, the vistas of fields and trees, the way the house snakes around like a story, not revealing the whole at any one time. And no room is too big or too small for what it is.

During lunch with my editor friend Joan Bingham, her remark about the value of writing fiction—"you get to know a lot of different kinds of people"—struck me with force. This might solve a certain lack of stimulation in Ashland.

There are times when Ashland seems like a desert of inactivity and my life without purpose or importance. The phone does not ring with pressing developments, people wanting my company. Maybe it never did. I am aware that most of what I imagine to be missing is an illusion. Everyone's life is full of potholes. Whoever I think of has to struggle to stay at the center of their own lives. When I think of the center of a wheel I wonder if dead center is, despite the turning outer rim, nearly still. That is the aim and object of meditation.

Norma in good form today. At Cross Brothers, to pick up a cantaloupe for breakfast, I decided to give her a recent compliment.

"Did you know that Pat Funk talked about you at the town council meeting last night?"

"That's what they say, that she mentioned my messages on the butter bean trays . . . but I tell people I haven't been in the right frame of mind lately."

"Oh?"

"There's been so much going on."

"Really?"

"My grandson tried to kill himself and my older daughter has cancer."

"What kind?"

"Lymphoma . . . the same kind that killed my daddy."

"Is your grandson her son?"

"No, he belongs to my son in Richmond. His wife just left him and she's had him arrested."

On it goes.

My backyard cottage is taking shape. Shingle men, window men, air-conditioning and heating men, plumbers, electricians. Trucks are continually pulling into the driveway. The buzz saw rings, the hammer pounds. It is very exciting.

Every day I visit the cottage at least a dozen times to plan my plans, dream its future. My latest idea is to offer it as part of a package—a writer's retreat and editing opportunity. When not being used by friends or family, a writer—I or another—can use it as a retreat.

The bay window is in. It feels as if the eye of the cottage has finally been inserted. Now when I walk inside it has focus and a sense of identity it didn't have before.

I can tell Mother is a little worried about her mental capacities. Recently she confused *sconce* with *scone* and wasn't sure which was which. Last night on the porch, talking with our friend Pat, she said, "Phyllie promised me she'd tell me when I should go mute."

There was never a time when I thought my mother had lost her mental acuity, although she used to joke about "brain cells flying out the window," and there were times when I could see her struggling for a word that was eluding her. I simply pretended not to notice. Then, too, she had been mangling the language forever, and when she got a word wrong it was much funnier and more interesting.

"That's meat for the fodder," she once declared. "Do you mean fodder for thought?" I asked. She blushed. "No, we're going to mix a little meat in it." Once, she said that something "shrieked her out," which admittedly is an improvement. And

upon returning from France, she reported that "stone argyles acted as rain gutters on the corners of the cathedrals.

But my favorite word mix-up was the time she wrote a letter to my friend Elizabeth, who was going through a hard time, and counseled, "Just remember, no one is free from immunity." If I knew how to needlepoint, that one would be on a cushion. "I don't know," said my mother, who knew she was wrong but still liked the way it sounded. "Every time I say it, it just flows."

Some thoughts on the troubled marriage of a friend: he is disdainful and cold, she is insecure and lacking in conversational rhythm when she is with him. There is a certain natural timing that is present when two people are at ease with each other. It is missing here. He begins to speak; she jumps in too fast.

A new thought—that writing is not only a reflection of what one thinks and feels but a rope one weaves with words that can lower you below or hoist you above the surface of your life, enabling you to go deeper or higher than you would otherwise go. What excites me about this metaphor is that it makes writing much more of a lifesaving venture.

IN ITALY AGAIN FOR MY FALL NIGHTWRITERS SEMINAR AT VILLA SPANNOCCHIA

The yearly miracle has occurred again. I am once more sitting in the dark morning before a newly lit fire in the villa living room. Two days of travel have ended with me fumbling for matches in Spannocchia's kitchen to make the first of a dozen cups of morning coffee. Now I open my journal and listen for my thoughts.

Last night, sitting with friends at an outdoor restaurant in Siena, on the street where Saint Catherine walked to her house a few feet from our table, I looked at the darkened town across the way, with its layered, stacked houses cut with golden squares of light.

It struck me how most of our conversation was conducted through stories. Gina told about the abduction of Saint Catherine's head by the Sienese, who demanded that the pope return her to Siena after her death in Rome; the pope had refused, so they snuck into the church where she was buried, lopped off the best part of her, plus a few fingers, and put them in glass cases that are still on display in the *duomo* here. Jennifer relayed her story of escaping from an alcoholic husband in Central America with her children, using forged documents, including a laundry ticket with some postage stamps as the final paper she offered to the border patrol soldier ("He read it upside down for several minutes and then waved us through"). She then told of a mutual friend's newly discovered talent for automatic writing (she sits down at her computer and her hands move without her bidding). I made them laugh with tales of different times I had pretended to be someone else—once an emergency room nurse, once a pediatrician—in order to help people who couldn't help themselves. All these stories were woven together into a disposable shawl that covered us just for that evening and then was discarded. We do this every time we meet.

❧

Today, one of my students said that she had stopped being polite because it wasted her time, to which another student asked, "And that works for you?" "Yes," she replied, after which the questioner fell silent. Falling silent should be cultivated, the way the woods fall silent in the snow. Messages you can't send any other way can be heard.

This is our third day together, and there is a sense of settling in that is making it easier for everyone to work. It is a very high-energy, motivated group. Katie and Kirstin are writing books. Christine is newly committed to a full-time writing life. Susan is a quiet deep-feeling person. Keke is awash in her own tumultuous life, leaking tears as she laughs over the details. Janet is charming and intense, Sharon blunt beyond the need for it but lovable nonetheless. Andy is overcome with joy, just at being here. Deb, the youngest, is innocently open to everything. Ruta is probably the most naturally talented and Judy the most hard-working and earnest.

Walking down the road from Cateni Restaurant at the top of the hill town of Orgia, I looked up into the sky. The air was full of dampness, chestnut smoke, and stars, with the soft verges of grass along the road smelling of *nipitella* mint and rain. What I need is some poetry to let me rub the moments between my fingers and release the scent.

Today I looked at one of my students who is giving me pangs of irritation and thought of a more compassionate way to view her—as someone usually so trapped in one small part of herself that it is difficult to experience the rest of her.

Our last day at Spannocchia. The small band that is left, only six, is softening fast now that the tougher, more judgmental members of the seminar are gone.

I wonder why I feel a magnetic attraction for this place when I am not exactly productive when here. The illusion, that I will be moving energetically from one brilliant place and conversation to another, is never matched by the reality of much sitting, eating, and feeling faintly bored. But at the same time I am watered, like a dry creek bed, with such beauty at every turn.

This morning, throwing open my shutters, the gold light on the wisteria, the pale sky mottled with pink clouds, the line of cypress trees along the terrace filled my eye. Now I am in a bar in Rosia, listening to the chatter of Italians having their morning cappuccinos. My heart simply loves this part of the world.

Home. Gazing at a small candle in a glass holder hanging from a chain—one of my purchases in San Gimignano that I knew would go in my writer's cottage behind the house. The pleasure I am taking from this work-in-progress, imagining the finished product, thinking of how it will be used and by whom, is continual. Watching carpenters put up solid beams of new wood, watching electricians fill the eaves with new wiring and pipes, all of it carefully done by craftsmen who know how to measure, plumb, and flesh out a line, is quietly thrilling.

Last night we had a wonderful warm dinner at the Lemons' house. Yet all of Virginia is in the grip of a grim lottery where almost every day someone is being picked off by a sniper. Last Saturday night, Ashland was the target. David Willis from Cross Brothers carried the victim to the hospital, but it could just as easily have been David; who was in the vicinity of the shooting only five minutes before it happened. Schools have been closed and parents are terrified to let their children play outside. Malls are empty. Nobody wants to risk being the next target, although the targets are so random— someone getting off a bus, a woman on a park bench, a child walking to school. It is impossible to know where to position oneself and the only real solution is to continue as if nothing significant could happen—the way we live, as if death were not the ultimate end for us all.

In his book *The Saints' Guide to Happiness,* Robert Ellsberg's reminiscence of his dying friend Chuck Matthei moves me:

To me [said Matthei, the last time Robert saw him] it is the recognition that we are never without a meaningful choice. This is a culture that nearly drowns people with meaningless consumer choices, yet leaves most of them feeling that they are powerless in the most important affairs of life—but that's not true. . . . This is the decision I have to make every morning: I can rise and think about what has been done to me, what I have lost . . . or I can rise and say to myself, "Here I am. Let's get moving!"

∾

A conversation with my sister, Cynthia, who has been visiting:

CYNTHIA: I like that magazine called *More*.

ME: I'd like a magazine called *Old*. Then I could go into a store and ask, "Have you got any *Old* magazines?" Or maybe there could be three different magazines called *Old*, *Older*, and *Oldest*.

MOM: Or *Finished*.

ME: Except who would buy it? Dead people don't read.

MOM: (changing the subject) I'm still aghast at someone having quadruple bypass surgery at eighty-seven. It shows what a tremendous fear of death we have.

∾

A Sunday morning. One candle burns rather noisily in the glass container that hangs from my new Italian "iron tree," and I am thinking that I have neglected the beauty that has been presented to me. When I could be writing about these things, I am browsing in dime stores, noticing and recording what isn't important.

Last night, the Moreland clan [whose father, Earl Moreland, lived the last part of his life here] descended on the house in a noisy, vivacious, piano-playing gang and instantly filled it with bright intelligence. Even Mother, who never contemplated a party she couldn't do without, was charmed to be there. Hearing the Moreland grandchildren banging on the piano while adults collared each other in conversation, with the smell of candles and coffee filling the air, I was back at my aunt and uncle's house in San Francisco, feeling the same kind of excited contentment that I felt then.

THINKING OF MOM

Think how it would feel, if I had an idea and because I was blind I could not pursue it. And, being old, I could not remember all the details. And being dependent upon someone else to stop and take the time to help me, I had to show great patience so that person would not become irritated with me.

I am beginning to look upon those who irritate me— the egoists, the overly emphatic, the nonstop talkers who press me against the wall—with more compassion. It is still a temptation to strike out and say something mean but true that will rip away their facades. But increasingly I am more inclined to look upon them as pilgrims who have gotten lost or forgotten where they are going, if they ever knew.

This thought was dislodged by a comment from Czeslaw Milosz:

William Blake was inclined to see human sins as phases through which humans pass and not as something substantial.
—*Milosz,* The Book of Luminous Things

It is time to rise and take some exercise. I wonder if I would do this more eagerly if I viewed my body as a friend who depended upon me, the way my mother does for her well-being.

A long talk with a distant friend fills you up like a meal full of comfort food. A hole is filled. This was how Franny Farr's call to me felt. My emotional stomach received solid nourishment, delighted by every morsel about her life and the lives around her.

❧

The other morning I shook an inchworm from my hair. It must have dropped off the dogwood tree when I stood beneath it snapping off a branch to decorate a room.

Back home, sitting at the breakfast table with the Sunday *New York Times,* I heard a little noise—the inchworm dropping onto the paper. It immediately headed for the paper's edge, bunching itself up like the eye of a hook and eye, sliding forward, bunching its little gray body up again. That something no larger than a tiny piece of string could be so purposeful and well-made caught my imagination and eye for the next fifteen minutes, which seems like a long time to give to a creature that small.

What interested me most was how the inchworm reacted to a new void. When it reached the edge of a section, say the Sports section, it paused thoughtfully, arched all but the anchoring end of its body off the page like a periscope, and looked around—or so I assume. It was too small to tell if it had eyes or perhaps tiny filaments, like hairs on a squirrel's tail, that "perceived" the situation. The inchworm would remain in this arched antigravity position for what seemed too long for such a minute organism to sustain. And then, carefully, it would lower its torso down, down, until it made contact with a new, lower surface. Then it would continue toward yet another challenge.

The Sunday *Times,* even when spread around, is like Mount Everest to an inchworm and eventually I got tired of watching it make its way from one part of the paper to the next. Putting my hand in its way, I let the inchworm crawl onto my finger and carried it outside, where I deposited it on the bush by the back door.

Numerous questions remain unanswered, like what and when does it eat? Average life span? But what interests me most is what is going on in that small intelligence as it poses, erect and thoughtful, for such a long time over the emptiness. Is it trying to decide whether the space is too wide and dangerous to challenge? And why does it never head for middle ground? Safety doesn't seem to play a big part in the inchworm's calculations. Not once did it strike out for the centerfold. This inchworm consistently headed for a fall.

Reading the first few pages of Harper Lee's *To Kill a Mockingbird* reminds me of how deeply imaginative a book can be. I want to write one like it. Her instinct for knowing what she can leave out may not be teachable, but the beginning of her book is a place to start.

This time of year is so spicy, with the earth not yet frozen and the leaves just beginning to fall. Rain soaks the ground, sending up smells of mold and mulch; the fires in people's houses mix with the cold air. Everything is coming to a head, with berries bright as blood in the magnolia cones, pumpkins in the field waiting to be carved up or to rot. I am enlarged, excited by it—if I don't think about the feudal state our country is becoming, in the hands of a president who dozed his way through good schools.

❧

It is consoling to think, if I am not always looking for God, that God is nevertheless looking for me. It is my suspicion, so deep that I forget its existence, that I am as profound as I am willing to be, that only a small revolution or turn toward the light would make all the difference.

❧

A dream in which I am talking on the phone with Christian while I wait to get into a limousine. I hang up and get into the car with all the family—Mom, Dad, Cynthia, all the aunts and uncles, plus Grandmother. We are taking Grandmother to a rest home. I sit next to her. She is quite calm and peaceful, with a smiling face. I take her hand and start to tell her how much she has meant to me and I begin to cry. Then the dream ends.

It is interesting that the importance of family in my value system has not created the family I wanted, that I used to love being in the midst of as a child. Yet perhaps the quiet and freedom I have and cherish is what I need, and that is what I have found.

❧

At 7:25 A.M. the first light touches the leaves of the sycamore tree outside the window. This is the most dazzling time of year.

The Riehls' Japanese maple tree is almost too beautiful to bear. The sugar in the leaves has turned them into brilliantly colored scraps of silk. One should be made to pay admission to see it.

This journal has been lost for a week. During that time I did little else other than think about my new book (writing to friends, sending e-mails) and my writer's cottage. Slowly, the inside is being finished up, like the last details of a child in the womb.

Last night, Mother unburdened herself of her frustration with me. Lying on the floor in front of the fire, she spoke of how every project she has is dependent upon my finishing it. It hurt to hear her quietly list the many requests I have repeatedly ignored: finding the Jennings appliance bill, addressing the envelope to Jennifer with the tapes, and so on. "I wonder if you can imagine not being able to use your fingers, for even a few hours," she said. "I look more competent than I really am." But most of all she said, "My creativity dies inside me."

The booklet of neighborhood resources that she has compiled is dependent upon me. Listening quietly, as she lay before the fire and talked, I was filled with remorse.

After she went to bed, I stayed up all night finishing the booklet so it could be taken to the printers and spiral-bound the next day.

Taking Mother to Peggy Siegel's office yesterday for an energy session was like taking a starving person to a meal. She was restored by it. She could talk to Peggy about her healing practices and exchange knowledge on a deeper level.

I first met Peggy when she came to one of my writing workshops in Ashland. A quiet, sensitive person who had not yet realized that she had special gifts, she wound up pursuing the profession of energy healer, studying under some of the country's most respected practitioners.

Later, Peggy told me that at the beginning of their session my mother had told her that she was really ready to cross over and did she think she was near to the time. Peggy said she didn't know, that she seemed really strong and healthy. What she didn't tell her was that my mother's energy was on such a high, fine vibration that Peggy kept getting dizzy. Then, toward the end of the session, Peggy saw an even more intense light fill up my mother's energy field. "Do you see it?" she had asked her. Mother said that yes, she did, and wondered what it meant. "You have an angel really close in, right with you," Peggy said. But neither of them knew how significant this was.

My long phone conversation with Robert Ellsberg and then reading aloud to Mother from his manuscript [*The Saints' Guide to Happiness*] last night was the gift of the day for me. We spoke of his life, his book, prayer (he used to do it effectively in the shower), and being distracted. The "mind at rest" is almost an oxymoron in this culture. Jonathan Franzen's book of essays on reading and the necessity of solitude for it is on the point we discussed.

Yesterday I was more aware of doing one thing at a time: eating without reading, walking without listening to a portable radio, doing my bills without having the television on, talking on the telephone without doodling. The day was more focused, I was more refreshed.

A way of looking at the importance of being educated: Every human being is born into the middle of a larger story. If we don't learn about the past, we won't know what happened before we got here and we will have greater difficulty making sense of what is happening now. It is like starting a book in the middle. It puts us at a disadvantage.

My session with Peggy Siegel: She asked me if I pray and to whom. I said that I had lost the impulse, that I was aware of being grateful, but not of directing it. When she opened her energy work by holding out her hands over me, she said she encountered a very crowded energy field, that there were many guides or spirits around me. She suggested that I ask them more specifically for guidance and help. The intention I asked for was to open my heart more. When she held her hand above my heart, it was as if tiny filaments were being brushed by the palm of her moving hand. She said there was a lot of energy coursing through my right arm.

This morning, on my way from Chestertown to New Jersey, I called Mom to see how everything was and my brother Tony answered the phone. "Phyllie, Mom's gone," he said. Just like that, the loving center of my life was no more—and I am writing this in a world where she will no longer be waiting downstairs every morning, bright-eyed and smiling, looking at me from behind her ravaged, all-seeing eyes. All I could think to ask Tony, beg him, was to not let anybody touch her until I got home.

I returned a few hours later and she was still sitting up in bed, where Tony had found her. I kissed her hands and cheeks and head—and cried my love to her, as this tiny pale face with the not-quite-closed eyes and slightly open mouth gazed unseeing upon the book with her teacher's picture on it that Tony had placed in her hands. She was wearing her down robe with Justin's cashmere shawl around her. From all appearances she was meditating and had simply, painlessly, slipped away.

I cannot define the feelings inside me at the present. When first I heard, I felt a tidal wave of tears; then a releasing of energy, too much to harness; then tears of love and gratitude, feelings of fear and freedom—all these things—but primarily gratitude, that she had been with me for so long.

When someone dies in a small southern town, the grief-stricken don't have to do anything but be bereaved. Mother's friend Reber dug the hole for a maple tree to be planted in her honor at the memorial service in the yard. My minister, who had not been asked to officiate, nevertheless showed up in a truck and quietly unloaded folding chairs on the lawn. Somebody went out and got a guest book. Flowers were arranged on windowsills and tables.

"I don't know how we're going to feed everyone," I said to my friend Pat.

"Don't worry," she said, "the food is in holding zones all over town." Sure enough, a half hour before the service began, *the women of Ashland came through the kitchen door, lugging pots of soup, casserole dishes, heaps of ham biscuits, and fruit bowls. By eleven o'clock, the lawn was full of people.*

The tributes were the service. No two were even vaguely similar. But the one I remember best came from a friend, Carolyn Key, who had recently visited with my mother on our back porch.

"I asked how she was," Carolyn described.

"Never one for small talk, she paused, taking the time first to listen, then to think. In a moment she replied, 'I'm free.'

"What do you mean, 'you're free'? I asked.

"'I'm free of any religious, philosophic, or political ideology, or anything else that ties me to this world.'

"On Sunday, when I heard of your mother's passing, I smiled—I don't think I've ever smiled before upon hearing of someone's death—because I remembered her words and knew that she was, indeed, free."

The service began with some Russian choral music and ended with Paul Simon's "Loves Me like a Rock."

The first morning after the funeral service, after Thanksgiving, after our visiting in Washington with my friend Elizabeth, Cynthia and I returned and tried to strip the living room and kitchen of the tonnage of flowers, mail, and food that had poured into the house since Mom died.

It feels as if the world, in all its bill-paying, saber-rattling, celebrity-attending selves, has drawn back. It is only the voices of my family and friends who can be heard.

As mildly shocking as it is to know that she is gone, she has left me free to make new choices that were not possible when she was here. Some of these choices are of the heart: to be more attentive to her friends and to my sister, Cynthia. Others are logistical. Do I want to move or stay in Ashland? I do not want this house to be underused or underoccupied.

But in these first days since the tide has pulled back from the shore, I want to be attentive to what I am seeing that had been hidden beneath my mother's life when she was here, the many, many people she touched, the bits and pieces of the mosaic that I was too close to, to see clearly at the time.

Yesterday, Cynthia and I worked on emptying Mom's room: her clothes and books and medicines, the large number of tapes. It was difficult work. Cynthia wept over her tiny tennis shoes. I felt sick, faintly, at the sight of her socks, underwear, and fuzzy orange sweater. Her range of interests hit me as I took her books off the shelf: everything from Khalil Gibran to *The Energy of Money*.

It keeps coming to me how I was unknowingly being prepared to play my part as the days grew closer to her final one. A week before I had paid all my bills, including December's mortgage, so I would not be encumbered by these necessities. Several days before her death, I had cleaned the dining room chandelier, replacing bulbs and adding shades so that the dining room sparkled for her service. I invited Peggy Siegel to the house, which meant that a day or two before Mom died she had a healing session with Peggy. And on a deeper level I had asked Peggy to open my heart. All around me are broken hearts. If I could ask for anything, it would be to have the love of truth that Mom possessed.

Cynthia and I marvel at the fact that the last warm day of autumn was the day of her service. From that day on it has been winter weather, the leaves racing in wind-driven packs across the yard. My little cottage comforts me.

This has been a week of radiance, of such great love pouring in the door. Last night the town turned out in force for my book party. It was the second time in six days that I had stood in front of so many dear, open faces, all of them shining with affection, and spoken to them of the love I have for this town. What an amazing fourteen years.

At the party, little Erika Dunkel took the coats, Sandy Shirey said she wants to make me a Christmas wreath (to show me, she said, "that the circle is unbroken"), Bobby Parker put his arm around me to say he was sorry about Mom, Sue Watson and Deering Gaddy made a contribution to the memorial fund, and someone I don't know hung an angel wind chime in Mom's tree. Patty Miller said the foot that Mom used to massage every Sunday doesn't hurt anymore. It could be, now that Mom is gone, that the healing she began on earth will intensify.

I am acutely aware of how the larger dynamic shifts when a person who played such a large role in one's life is gone. My mother had always been the primary relationship in my sister's life. Now, for my relationship to my sister to grow I must change, and it will be a challenge. Already I'm trying to change her in ways to suit me! And I can be so mean it takes me aback.

Pat is a rock, miraculous in itself. Cynthia, too, is surprising herself. She has been preparing for this day for a long time and compares herself to a tree, losing all its leaves but finding beneath them that she is intact, with a strong trunk and branches. This is a beautiful metaphor for the grief she feels.

❦

The first night of being home by myself was softened by Dorothy's nieces, Sandra and Sarah, who always came for a foot rub by Mom on Wednesday night. They arrived with dinner, which we gobbled with glee. Later, after they had left, Pat arrived, and we sat by the fire talking about how we felt about Mom not being here. "I miss her," said Pat, "but there's not that longing I've felt when other people have died."

There is snow in Ashland, lovely snow, and I am surrounded by loving neighbors on every side. What I feel about this community and my life here is that the level of realness and beauty is very high.

Last night was the first time I began to feel the loneliness of Mom's absence. There is no one to cook for, have a drink by the fire with, or to tell funny stories about Norma, who sent the following condolence card to me today:

I know you will miss your mom. This time of year is even worst. My mom is still here but her mind isn't. It's not the same. Since my sister died a year ago, I just don't enjoy things anymore. You are a dear friend and I wanted to wish you a wonderful Christmas and lots of luck on your writing.

There is a sweetness about Norma that is deeper than her gloom—but barely.

Conversation with my friends is deeper since Mother died. Carol came with lunch yesterday and a book of spiritual readings, one of which she read as a blessing before we ate. Last night, by the fire, Reber, Pat, and I talked about how Mom was a person who shone light into other people's lives. Reber told a story from a Robert Fulghum book about a man who used to ask people what they thought the purpose of life was. He was always laughed at until one time he was in Greece and he asked the question of an Orthodox priest after his sermon. The priest said, "I'm glad you asked. For me the answer is found in an experience I had as a young shepherd. One of my sheep had gotten lost, and I searched all over until I came to a cave. I couldn't see into it but I had a bit of metal and I angled it to reflect the sun and the rays lit up the interior, where I saw the lamb in the back of the cave. Since then I have thought that this is what I want to do—shine light into other people's lives."

We agreed that this is what Mom did.

The phrase "alone in the world" gathers force as you age. Last night, I lay in bed upstairs, aware that the bottom floor was empty and it felt like a cold slab on my back. I am not being warmly supported from below. Searching my mind for other sources of support, I think of my closest friends who are like flower bulbs, growing at different rates and in different parts of my life. We do not do well apart from community, but we need to take our real nourishment from within.

Talking with my brother Tony last night, I compared the feeling I have to that of graduating from one school and entering another. There is a feeling of newness and anxiety and excitement. As for missing Mom, I cannot miss what I feel I have, and I continue to be glad that she didn't have to wait any longer to get out of "school" when she had completed her work.

❧

Last night, I was filled with a kind of loving pity for my mother. She was so small and unprotected and innocent, and for all her strengths she was still such a young and tender soul when she died. I was swept away by the thought of her largely unattended life. Yet her death has made me acutely attentive. The whole town seems to have been startled into a wakefulness that is new. Reber said last night that an enlightened person raises the level of consciousness of the entire community. I think this has happened.

❧

In Washington, walking down Connecticut Avenue, I watched a flock of birds rise up into the sky like a dark quilt that moved swiftly through the air as if it were being shaken. Then they drifted up against the side of a building and perched like metal icebreakers on the roofline. What kind of intelligence connects them?

❧

It occurs to me, as I think of Peggy Siegel, that the most deeply lived lives are also the most interesting—and dramatic.

Yesterday, Peggy offered me three healing sessions in honor of my mother and then, when I was lying on the table, said almost casually that she could be in touch with her while we were together. She felt Mom in the room when I entered and said she was in and out—a stronger or weaker presence—throughout the session. At one moment, while listening for her, Peggy giggled. "What's so funny?" I asked. "I don't know if this can be her," she said. She listened some more and giggled again. "She says she really digs bilocation." I was oddly unmoved—unaffected—by this and, while not disbelieving, I was not believing either.

Peggy advised me to "notice" my body more, that it was the route to my spirit, or words to that effect. I said I felt well. "You are!" she said. But I continue to be unable to feel the sensation, or see the colors or images that some people feel in their sessions with her. Only warmth at the point of contact, or a feeling, faint but pleasant, of being replenished, or filled. "She left you full" is how Peggy spoke of Mom when I told her that I always felt that way about Mom when she wasn't around.

A lightheadedness yesterday. I called my friend Debbie, and the warmth and reassurance I associated with Mother came pouring through the phone. Later I called Justin. He said he would be coming down to be with me for Christmas. I wept when I spoke to him.

From Mother's journal/book:

What keeps you from being fully alive is what you are most afraid to go through. —Lawrence McCafferty

Without discrimination and renunciation, the energy of your prayer or ecstasy will be momentary, like a sizzling drop of water on a redhot iron pan, all sound and no substance. —Ramakrishna

Under every moment of anger is an enormity of sadness, and under that a sea of compassion. —Stephen Levine

> *You have a duty to perform.*
> *Do anything else, do any number*
> *Of things, occupy your time fully.*
> *And yet if you do not do this task,*
> *All your time will have been wasted.*
> —Rumi

A wonderful visit from my friend Katie Roeper last night. She talked about how, when her own mother was dying, she had asked Katie if she wanted her to come to her after she was gone. And Katie, then in her teens, had reacted negatively, at which her mom had backed off and said, "Okay, I'd never do anything that would scare you." But Katie feels it's just a question of being open to it, letting oneself be present to the possibility.

A call from Julie Beck, who felt Mom's presence so strongly in *Giovanni's Light*. She wanted to call me after her death. Then she read the book and had to call.

It came to me yesterday that our life does not fully flower until it is over. Its final meaning can't be known until after we are gone. Written down, this makes it sound as if the worth of a life is weighed by the number of people who remember us. But I mean something more, which is connected to the new life my mother is leading now. Her power has intensified, rather the way a saint's efficacy is spread.

A dream last night about Mother. She was sitting across a table, telling me about her death. "My death wasn't ugly or traumatic, so Hollywood doesn't want it," she said. In my dream I picked up a pencil and wrote this down.

AT SAINT STEPHEN'S CHURCH IN RICHMOND WITH THE BLANCHARDS FOR CHRISTMAS LESSONS AND CAROLS

The faces of the choirboys from Saint Christopher's were so open and elegant, their features smooth and firmly carved. Looking at them fed my heart. All around me were Richmond's most fortunate, and I cannot say I felt distinct or different. A lifetime of privilege, driving down streets tastefully strung with Christmas lights, instead of streets that are shabby and run-down, protects me from a great deal.

It is not yet a month since Mom has gone. I continue to be carried by a peace that Dorothy Jones aptly said she "didn't hardly think could be had in this world." It is a peace that those who were closest to her share.

DECEMBER 21, 2002

Winter solstice, a day Mom loved. The light is never farther from the Earth, and every day henceforth it will come closer.

My house is ready for Christmas, the mantel and windowsills decorated with fir branches, lights and candles, a wreath on every door and window, the fireplace set with wood.

Whenever I think of Mom, I can't help feeling somewhat inferior to her. By temperament and spiritual habits, she was more refined than I am. It would not make her happy for me to be thinking this way, and I am, in fact, grateful that she left behind such an astonishing life to emulate and love. But it is daunting to feel that so large a mountain remains for me to climb. By slipping over the top, she compels me to follow.

Last night I had a date with a man who left me bored. I do not realize how much I live in a world of ideas and literature until I spend time with someone who doesn't. And it didn't help that after a while he began to look like Vice President Cheney. I am lamentably, immovably, at the center of my own life, and it would take a great love to alter my position. Yet I wish one would present itself. My heart has a capacity for love that is not being used.

The notion of not wanting to be in charge of my life interests me now that I feel I am. For so many years, more than half my life, I struggled with the emotional belief that if I could rest secure in the love of a partner I would blossom, like a flower well and truly planted. The idea that I had soil enough of my own took a long time to mature.

2003

In Carmel, California

A winter walk on the beach this morning with my old college friend Judy McDonald. We talked about her poetry, our families, and the ways in which we grow. Stewart's Beach was awash in morning light, the gulls lifting like a net of wings, when the ocean waves purled toward them, wheeling by the hundreds above my head without ever colliding. What pilot could navigate so well? I collected twisted pieces of driftwood (future drawer handles) and pitched bread pellets at the terns, remembering how I used to take Christian here before he could walk. He would crawl across the sand toward the gulls and gurgle with delight when they flew up in a sudden rush over his head when he got too close to them. It was his first experience of his own power, and it delighted him.

Today, lunch with Francesca's friend Annabelle Lund, who is always doing the unheard-of thing. Recently, she returned from Bosnia, where she had commandeered an ambulance and made dozens of trips out of the war zone, ferrying children to safety. She didn't speak Serb or Croatian, she just faked her way through all the checkpoints. I asked her what early influences made her the person she is today.

"My parents," she replied. "They taught me that if you have an eye for other people's suffering, you have an obligation to do something about it that other people who don't see it don't have."

"You can lose the ability," I said.

She nodded. "It can atrophy."

Home again: The weekend was a lonely one. Mom was insulation. Always she was in another room, within earshot, available to hear my last thought. Without her, it would be particularly good to hear from my children, yet they are silent and I am pushed back upon myself and the knowledge that one's happiness and worth must come from within.

Children are markers of our mortality, reminding us of how far along the road we are. But they are on very different parts of it. While I sit alone before the fire wishing the phone would ring, they are having supper with a lover, deciding whether to be married, feeling the urgency of getting on with it so they can have their own children. To be asked to give mothering to a mother is difficult for them to imagine, much less do, until they are older, closer to the age I am now.

Snow again! The power company won't come today. My little unheated cottage continues to wait for light, heat, and life. How impatient I am to see it done. All the kitchen drawers are full of pots, dishes, dishcloths, and silverware. But nothing more can be done, including laying down the final floor covering, until the Almighty Power Company comes to town.

❧

I am writing an essay for a magazine. The words don't shine but they are what come to the surface—small fish while the large ones move silently in the depths, waiting.

❧

A note about friendship—one Ashland friend in particular. Over the years, Ellen Papoulakos has expanded in my mind like a painting that I had only seen the corner of, and the closer I looked the more was revealed. Yesterday, spending an hour with her when my electricity was off, was a joy. She is smart and honest and deep-feeling, with such a wonderfully incisive humor. She hurts terribly when her girls give her grief. But even in the telling of a harrowing teen tale, she makes me laugh. The hour we spent together stayed with me all day. She really feels like a friend one can grow with. Like her house, her spirit is large, solid, and full of light.

❧

I am reading a book about Buddha. He was called the Awakened One. I think that I am still largely dreaming, but the images in my dreams are becoming sharper. Perhaps this is a step.

❧

Yesterday I returned the cards I had bought at the local stationery store to acknowledge all the condolence notes I received after Mom's death—to exchange for others I liked more. "You know how up in the air one gets with a death," I told the young store owner. She nodded sympathetically. Then, when she added up the total of the new cards, she said it came to a little more but never mind. "How much?" I asked. "Thirteen fifty" she said. "That's not a little more!" I exclaimed. "You'll be going out of business if you act this way." "But I am," she said, and then she told me that she had just been diagnosed with breast cancer.

More snow! I am beginning to feel like a character in *Giovanni's Light*. It is dark and frozen and, save for the light from the woodstove, cheerless. I am feeling adrift without Mom here.

The weekend in Washington was a respite from the loneliness I can feel in Ashland. Seeing my old friend Huston delighted me. He has a slight stoop, almost undetectable, when he walks. His hair is now gray and a bit thinner, but the same vitality is there, the same humor and quickness. He worries about getting old. Now is the time to do what he has put off. Huston's politics are conservative and top down, rather like that of a dog trainer who knows that firmness is always the answer. He supports Bush and thinks our mistake was not getting rid of Saddam in the Gulf War. We agreed to disagree. On a deeper level it is easy for us to converse.

What is troubling me now is the external lack of connections in Ashland. All the life that poured through the front door when Mother was here seems to have almost completely stopped. It wasn't a lot—the little honking sounds as Esther and Dorothy pulled up to take Mom to the cemetery;

her friends, like Pat and Reber, stopping by—but now it has stopped. I am the mistress of a quiet, orderly universe with nothing except myself to remind me that I am here.

I wonder if the death of those we love prepares us for our own. The pull of those who have gone before us gives us reasons to welcome the end of our life as the prelude to a reunion.

Yesterday I read a sentence in a story by Isak Dinesen: "He was, he thought, the loneliest being in the world." It consoled me, as if knowing of another who felt the same way diminished the feeling in myself. Then, while alphabetizing the books in the writer's cottage, the feeling of *wanting* to be alone set in. So there is a place, deeper than loneliness or being with others, that is neither one nor the other—and as I sorted books I glimpsed it. Solitude.

Last night, after rehearsing for the Ashland Variety Show, I walked back to the car thinking how the fact that I am loved is not in doubt. But it is the proximity of that love that comforts us. After a while it is of no use to count up all our family and friends in far-off places. The need to love and be loved close up is still there.

Later, after midnight, I heard a knock on the front door. It was the man who had just cut my grass that afternoon. He was reeking of alcohol and said he needed gas money so he could "pick up a loan of $2,500." I told him to come back tomorrow and we would talk about it. He knew I wasn't buying his story and he backed off into the night. Thinking of this small well-made man, who had worked with such vigor on my yard all afternoon, drifting through the dark streets, breaking his mother's heart, is like a sad song no one hears. Before I went to bed, I bolted the doors and set chairs against them, even though I knew he was harmless.

Now it is morning, which restores my heart. I feel quietly full of possibility.

My last visit with Larry Blanchard, eighty-three, who is near death. He lay small and collapsed on his big hospital bed, his cold hand holding hard to my warm one. His wife, Frances, is a formal woman, but she kissed me good-bye when I left and said, "I love you." It is amazing how real love can melt reserve.

An innocent question from someone at the gym—"Still writing?"—caused me to strike out. "Why do people ask that?" I shot back. "I'm a writer. That's what I do." She was embarrassed and taken aback and I regretted my words instantly. But they were out, like a snake that has struck a victim, before I could control myself. Then my own embarrassment, or shame, set in.

I have been continuing to study the writing of Jacques Lusseyran. His capacity to see, although he was blind, depended on his ability to pay attention—neither going forward too much nor wanting anything from the object of his attention, so that the thing could impress itself upon him.

Recently I discovered an unidentified mass at the base of my neck on the left side. I went in for an X-ray and then waited for the results from my doctor. Every time the phone rang or I saw the red light flashing saying a message was waiting, I said to myself, "The truth is my friend." This helped a lot. Then the verdict: I have a goiter and the doctor wants me to start on thyroid supplements.

Prior to hearing the news, I was clearing a huge stash of books out of a wooden chest, and when the chest was empty I saw something gray at the bottom. Reaching down to pick it up, my hand felt fur and I gave a small shriek. It was a mouse, years old. I thought, *The truth is my friend. So it's a dead animal. The world is full of them. There is nothing repulsive about that. It's all conditioning.* This was how I talked to myself as I went into the kitchen to get a pair of rubber dishwashing gloves. Walking back into the living room, I reached down into the box, closed my hand around the furry object, and brought it into the light. It was a mouse toy! The truth really *is* my friend.

A long heartfelt conversation with Eliza. At one point we were both in tears. She had wanted so much to be close to me when she was growing up, yet I was not strong enough to pierce the firewall she erected between us when she was a teenager. We talked about forgiveness. "It means giving up on trying to change the past," she said. And then she spoke of losing her biological mother. Yet in losing her, she said, she found me. This is when she began to cry, as did I. If I had to choose I would have our story begin sadly and end happily, but how deeply I mourn for the little girl who needed so much more than I knew how to give.

Yesterday was the first warm day of spring. I feel as if I am in a new skin, that every frozen thing has been unlocked and made over. In front of me on the coffee table is a bunch of daffodils. I can hardly take my eyes off them. Each crisp yellow head bursts out from the stalk, clean, clear, and fragrant.

Why I have changed I don't know, but order is a new, seemingly easy habit for me these days. When Mother died, she left her meticulousness behind. Every other day a new bag of things for Goodwill is loaded into my car.

"I miss your mother!" exclaim many of her Ashland friends when I run into them. It is a natural remark, but it is the comparison that hurts, knowing that I am not my mother and that her friends are thinking this, too, comparing me to her and wishing I could be exchanged for her. This is a terrible self-pitying hole to fall into and I am not sure how to get out.

Then Pat called and I tried to describe my state of mind. She understood and commiserated. A few minutes later, Katie telephoned, wanting to have lunch. She had her own troubles, so the two of us sat in my kitchen and shared our lives with each other and were lighter because of it. Later, I kept my appointment with Peggy, and she ran energy into me as I mostly slept. But she was very confirming and urged me to focus upon receiving so that my capacity to give would remain in balance. "Try to be aware of your mother's presence," she said. "It's subtle, but you can sense it if you are open to it." Even the mention of Mother filled my eyes with tears. And finally at the end of the day, Carolyn Hemphill sat by the fire and kept me company. When I look back at this one day there was a lot to receive.

One of the day's highlights was a long satisfying conversation with my friend Kerin. She told me a story about her husband, Patrick. They have three very challenging children as well as a difficult dog. One day Kerin said to Patrick that the dog was too much to handle on top of everything else that was going on and that he had to go. But Patrick said he didn't think that was a good message to send to the children, given the fact that they were adopted—that when a dog is difficult it is given away. "We'll just say that it's a member of the family and we'll deal with it."

She read me a letter she received from the writer Carol Bly on the subject of dealing with the vicissitudes of life:

For your own sake I feel pleased you are shedding, one by one or perhaps for all I know ten thousand by ten thousand, those feelings of being entitled not to suffer this thing or that in life—such as mental illness in one's immediate family. It is such a good thing for a writer to lose all feelings of having any rights to a decent life. Here is why: If one has no rights or expectations with regard to a decent life, no immunities, one's heart overflows with gratitude. That gratitude is a handy place from which to write.

A new calm is upon me. I am fed by the companionable quiet of the early morning. *Work,* it says. *Draw closer. The way is prepared for you.*

I find my reaction to other people's troubles and joys instructive. My sister's new lover has made her calm and solicitous of me, and I don't like it. The role I was in the habit of playing—of the wiser, more sophisticated older sibling—has been taken from me by my younger sister, and it doesn't suit me at all to be robbed of my "power." When we become attached to a role for our identity, it is very hard to give it up. But if the play is to keep going, we can't get too attached to our parts, as they keep changing.

Larry Blanchard's funeral in the First Presbyterian Church in Richmond was brilliant. His son Buck's tribute was just like Larry—authoritative, funny, and wistful. The sanctuary was packed. I found myself weeping with the singing but truly joyful that Larry was finished with his work. And then my tears were for the deep sadness in life. I wept for my children who were hurt by all my broken promises to them. I wept for other children weeping because their parents had let them down.

The amount of time and effort I put into getting dressed for his funeral seems like a superficial reaction to such a deep event. Applying cosmetics to heighten the color of my face and cheeks made me feel as if I were a corpse myself. Women applying makeup are like morticians fixing up the dead.

An item in *Newsweek* about the phenomenon of aging and how a certain chemical, GABA, keeps us sharp. As we age the brain does not produce as much and our capacity to filter out distractions and noise decreases, making it more difficult to learn. What the article doesn't discuss is why the brain does this. Is there some benefit to the decrease?

∾

The Ashland writing seminar begins tonight. The house is in readiness—washed floors, cleaned rugs, polished furniture, jugs of white peonies on every table, at every window. The last hours before my students' arrival will be spent working over the exercises, putting their folders in order.

The blessings in my life increase: the steady love of friends, the material support of income, good health, interesting work, and the amazing rewards of family. Eliza is coming for ten days, which seems miraculous. And I am also aware of a new kind of undeserved ease in my life, with tasks being accomplished and goals reached with so little strain that I practically float from one to the other. This morning, as I often do, I looked at the book of my mother's writings that I put together for her funeral. "Innocence is the capacity to be found" she copied on one page. That was certainly her.

When I feel empty and dissatisfied, with more time than ways to use it, my first impulse is to fill my life with other people. But this is precisely when I should not do this. Equal relates to equal, and my imbalance would throw the other person into a state of imbalance, too

Happiness consists of such small things: a glance in the mirror that makes one feel attractive, a clean shirt, the prospect of a friend for lunch. When I came into the dining room I saw the phone flashing with a message. It turned out to be my granddaughter, Rhys, pouring her four-year-old heart out into my answering machine. I could only understand a third of it, but it was so sweet to hear.

When all is said and done, everything we're given or learn or possess in any real sense—the ability to play Beethoven sonatas, write books, understand the principles of physics—is intended for one thing: to draw us closer to our selves. When I think of how the vast stores of knowledge a human brain contains are destroyed at death—all of I. F. Stone's Greek, his love of dancing with his wife, Esther—then I have to conclude that he was given these things, like walking sticks, to support him on his pilgrimage.

The obvious occurs to me: If you don't consider your life a pilgrimage, it gets downgraded to a trip or even an aimless journey. It is we who make that decision.

Yesterday was Mom's birthday. I found myself thinking about my good friends dying, and it was comforting to realize that it will happen to us all. It is not comforting to think about my children dying. I think this is because I want to be there when they go.

My house is like an exterior brain, storing memories that sometimes slip out between the folds—like the bound collection of funeral tributes for the writer Otto Friedrich that fell onto the carpet from under the ledge of a cabinet in my living room. Molly [his daughter] had sent them to me eight years ago. This morning I read them, some for the first time.

In 1955, when I was preening myself over one of the infinitely few fan letters that accompanied the publication of my first novel, Otto observed, "Those are the people who come after you in the middle of the night with an ax." —William Gaddis

History is about the passion of thought and the will to understand, about Darwin sailing for the Galapagos or Dostoevsky in trouble with the police, about Otto Friedrich, sick or in pain, blind in one eye, playing Bach's Partita in C Minor on a winter night on a piano badly out of tune, planning his next raid on the kingdom of the past, wondering how he might hearten himself and his fellow men with a story not yet told. —Lewis Lapham

Otto is gone, but these words about him will live as long as there are readers.

My brain is not the agile athlete it used to be. The same name can get lost and find itself a dozen times a day. But we are saved by the brains of others who remember for us. Over the phone, Lucy Childs told me a story I relayed to her nine years ago (who could remember that?) about teaching in a women's prison and asking the class to create a family tree. One inmate wrote a date and, after it, noted: THE DEATH OF MY PARENTS. Of course I sympathized with her, saying how hard for her that must have been to lose them both on the same day. She nodded, with lowered eyes. Only later did I find out that she was in prison for plotting their murders.

Yesterday, coming home from errands, I had a new feeling of actually being glad that Mom had gone, that she didn't have to endure her aged body, her shredded eyes, the oppressive heat of summer in Virginia. I also had to concede that her death was good for me. I have the freedom to move at will from one place to another now. There is also the feeling that she is in the wings, effecting some of the changes that are happening now, like my sister getting engaged.

Looking out at my unmowed lawn and unweeded flower beds, a thought that seems new occurs to me. When I don't want to know something unflattering about myself (in this instance that I am not a good gardener), my first instinct is to go to a friend and ask if this is true, hoping they will say no. But not so fast. Isn't it better to sit with my suspicions and examine them over the next few days and answer that question for myself? I might discover something valuable that a friend's desire to be kind would deny me.

Little by little, the truth in the family whose oral history I am taking down is emerging. The grandmother's diary alludes to the lack of love in her marriage, a son tells of the gardener being his steadiest childhood companion, a daughter talks of being the family scapegoat. Everyone in the family is dying for love—and forgiveness.

Thinking about forgiveness, I recently heard of a shocking custom in a primitive tribe. When someone in the tribe has killed another member, they strap the dead victim onto the murderer's back until he eventually dies, too.

The Bible says, "He who hates his brother is a murderer. The man who does not love is among the living dead." When we hold something in our heart against someone and will not forgive, we actually hate the person and that hatred binds us to them just as surely as love does.

Medical findings indicate that bitterness and lack of forgiveness can bring on all manner of diseases. Could it be that those we hate, and thus murder spiritually, are bound to us, slowly poisoning our own souls until we are among the living dead? This is a serious consideration, especially in the light of the fact that in Greek the word *forgive* means *to unbind*.

Up very early, 4:30 A.M. Troubled dreams in which I do not fit anywhere, can't find the right clothes or place to be. I feel like the parents in Jonathan Franzen's novel, *The Corrections*. I am losing it, slowly but surely, word by word. So I get up to be with myself, even though I feel in need of sleep. I never knew how much of an anchor my mother was until she died. We were like geese, mated for life. And now that I am alone, I am stumbling over the emptiness, trying in vain to fill it by leaving town, and the price is too great.

Outside, the dark is filled with birds talking in soft cheeps, signifying another reality just as valid as my own. Sitting here, my strength returns, the way the presence of an old friend makes us whole.

NOTES ON MY VISIT WITH MOLLY W, WHOSE ORAL HISTORY
I AM JUST BEGINNING

The time with Molly was a tonic. She is an admirable woman.
At eighty-two she walks with a firm spirit and step and there
is not an ounce of self-pity in her. Neither is there much room
for reflection. She has survived by not looking too far beneath
the surface, by her own admission. She loved her mother
and maternal grandmother deeply and wants the book we
are writing to preserve and vindicate their lives. Yet it will
require some more reflection from Molly to do it right, as
her mother and grandmother left little of themselves to draw
from, other than a few photographs and, in her mother's case,
several diaries filled with what she did and with whom. After
reading Molly's mother's journal, mostly about where she
ate and shopped, mine seems like a biographer's dream, not
nearly as vapid as I feared.

I love a broad margin to my life. —*Thoreau*

Yesterday was a perfect summer day. All the earth was perfectly moist, the weeds came up easily, the grass glistened,
and I spent nearly all day outside planting flowers, pulling up
lamb's-quarter, and reclaiming the garden. It is beginning to
have a luxuriant cared-for look. And even though, at various
times during the day, I realized that I was alone and should
perhaps be uneasy over this, I dismissed the thought as unwor-
thy of the day itself.

Sometimes it feels as if the relationships with my children are suffering a kind of gradual death by neglect or lack of

communication. Yet when I consider the alternatives, I don't see any that are better. Do I want them to live with me or me with them? Do I want to reclaim my old position at the center of their lives? No. What I want is to be at the center of mine, and yesterday, all day, I was.

The notion of not wanting to be in charge of my own life interests me now that I feel I am. For so many years, more than half my life, I struggled with the emotional belief that if I could rest secure in the love of a partner I would blossom, like a flower well and truly planted. The idea that I had soil enough of my own took a long time to mature.

I am doing some hard thinking, and Thoreau is helping me:

I was thinking, accidentally, of my own unsatisfactory life, doing as others do; and with the vision of the diggings before me, I asked myself why I might not be washing some gold daily, though it were only the finest particles—why I might not sink a shaft down to the gold within me, and work that mine.

This long, delayed summer lies around me like a perfumed lake, the trees thick with leaves and birds, every field loaded with daylilies, foxglove, and Queen Anne's lace. The most important truth to accept is that we are continually changing. The daylily I snip for a kitchen jug is on its way to extinction. As the Buddhists teach, we must imagine the glass in our hand as already shattered.

My days have been full of small things: choosing paint colors, cleaning out kitchen shelves, arranging for doctors' appointments. Yet there is a harmony to them, a feeling of anticipation, as if I am readying a ship for a long trip for which I have neither destination nor itinerary.

Yesterday I heard the story of how bald eagles, when they get old, stop eating, and if it weren't for the younger eagles who bring them food they would die. But then they are given new life and come out of their decline stronger than before. It is the way I feel about my children's importance in my life. One needs to be around young people or you lose something very important.

Yesterday, my chief joy came from spending several hours with Peggy, working on her autobiography. Then an hour on Ellen's front porch with a gin and tonic, followed by a stop at Mary Lou Brown's and a long porch talk with Conde Hopkins. I felt rooted in my life, lacking in nothing that is not provided.

In Charleston, South Carolina, staying with my friend Nikki, who was stunned to realize that I had recently signed up on Match.com. I told her I was somewhat stunned myself, but it was an easy entertaining way to see who was available in different zip codes, without even having to comb your hair. We decided to look at the men on Match.com around Charleston. As each new man came onto the screen Nikki would editorialize.

"*Loves to cuddle.* Cuddle? No, I would want to get to work.

"Christian? Out!

"Sullivans Island. He's rich. But what does he have on his head, a woman's hat? Enlarge his photo. Oh, my God, he's on a horse. One of those dressage types. No way!

"A southern gentleman. Oh, no, that's out. I hate southern men. He probably has a belt with a Confederate flag on it.

"Look, he's eating a pizza! What kind of person would have a picture of himself eating pizza?"

I haven't been here long enough to feel Charleston in my bones, but the summer air is soft and slow moving. On Wadmalaw Island, the live oaks are hung with moss, ivy climbs up the tree trunks and ribbons of water wrap the land into separate islets. There is something reassuring about being in a place pulled back and forth by the tides. You can see the land respond, the water move. The beach on Sullivans Island is a Prendergast oil, with clouds and pelicans and necklaces of bright green tendrils with white morning glories casting a net across the sand. This is beautiful country. More and more I understand why Southerners prefer one another's company and culture. There are fewer sharp edges.

Nikki's house is like her: small, shiny, and intelligent. Coke bottle cap crucifixes, postcards of Marilyn Monroe, white Christmas lights and seashells on the front porch. The fever of having me, or anyone, here seemed to have broken last night. I could sense, at dinner, that she was finally relaxed. We talked about writing, ideas for columns, and books.

Through Match.com I made a coffee date with a Charleston man. But I think I've caught the cyberdating wave too late. He is not my idea of anything except a man with fixed ideas and bad bridgework. I do not feel that old or broken down, and never could I imagine being physically intimate with him or anyone like him. My present life seems so much more expansive.

Nikki is right. Growing old together lessens the shock of meeting someone old for the first time. The married couple in front of us in the movie house was rosy and overfed. Like two cows in a field, they have aged together, and daily proximity has softened the reality. Perhaps they are bored beyond belief with each other and the contents of their lives, but they have each other in the movies, and that—for many people who are afraid to be alone—is the point.

Okay, so maybe this entry about going online to look for a relationship took you by surprise. That makes two of us. All I can say is that I am 50 percent embarrassed about it and 50 percent not. But as decisions go, this one didn't have a lot of lead time. One night, sitting in front of the upstairs television watching Entertainment Tonight *(now that's embarrassing) while ironing a stack of napkins, onto the screen came a former "bachelor" from that now-defunct reality show to talk about his new job—as the PR representative for Match.com. I listened to his spiel, turned off the iron, and walked across the room to my computer to log on. By the end of the week, I had written a brief autobiography, selected a recent photograph (taken at my older son's wedding), and joined up.*

What I liked about Match.com was the ability to pick a zip code and see who was available. I trolled the west side of New York, the Monterey peninsula, all of Marin, the Georgetown section of Washington, D.C., Montana—what about Billings, or maybe Missoula? It was fun. Then I hopped across the Atlantic to Europe, but the language barrier got in my way. Still, for an extrovert who feels a little restless in a small town, it was great entertainment, tinged with hope.

My life did not change. There were a couple of men I thought looked interesting, and I e-mailed them but got no reply. Maybe they were plants, put there by Match.com to dress up the stag line. I had lunch with a really nice professor from a nearby university who was an avid bike rider, but I outweighed him, and I just don't think he could imagine me pedaling along-side. And once I wrote someone back and said I didn't think we were a match (I think he was a retired soybean farmer on the Eastern Shore of Maryland), but I knew someone he might like. He must have been insulted as he never wrote back.

I was actively involved in this mostly virtual dating scene for about three months, and then I got bored and went on to other things. But my membership was for six months, which turned out to be a good thing.

Yesterday afternoon, the sun shattered a jug of hydrangeas into shards of light on my dining room table. It was there for anyone to look at but I only did so in passing, the way a king glances casually out the carriage window at his kingdom.

An overnight at the Blanchards' house on the river. I loved the small brown birds in the oak trees by the back deck. They fell from branch to branch as silently as drops of water, small and adorable, no bigger than plump figs.

Buck admitted that his father's death had given him a greater sense of confidence. He is no longer his father's son. When he goes to people in the community as a businessman, the background tapestry of his father's living presence is no longer there. I can see how important it is that our parents die. That we die. The field would be too crowded; the ability of our children to extend themselves in all directions would be too limited.

Tobias's birthday. Seven! He is such a remarkable and remarkably loving boy.

A second grandson [Christian, Jr.] will be here within the next twenty-four hours. The whole family is keeping watch from coast to coast.

The baby came last night around seven. In California. He is perfect and calm, a little boy who lies in his mother's arms looking at the world with quiet curiosity. Unspoken but real is the fact that he is not damaged in any way.

Christian's love of his baby is bringing new feelings to the fore. "How could anybody be mean to my child?" he asked.

I am reading Arthur Miller's autobiography, *Timebends,* which is quietly astounding me. Everything he examines becomes vivid and poignant at the same time.

On his mother:

She was a woman haunted by a world she could not reach out to, by books she would not get to read, concerts she would not get to attend, and above all, interesting people she'd never get to meet.

On the playwright Clifford Odets:

Odets seemed to me to share something of Marilyn's special kind of perceptive naïveté; like her, he was a self-destroying babe in the woods absentmindedly combing back his hair with a loaded pistol.

On artistic failure:

In American theater the quickest route to failure is success, and if you can't get there yourself, there are plenty around who'll be happy to give you a lift.

The disconnections between what I believe and how I live are almost too numerous to mention: I abhor hunting and eat meat, consider myself someone who doesn't care about material things but take way too many trips to the mall, think television has a terrible effect on the imagination but go to sleep with it on, love solitude except when I'm on the phone.

Yesterday I had one of those chance conversations that light up my imagination. A writer from Austin, Texas, called about my seminars and cottage. She told me that her parents had been circus performers from Tuscany who emigrated to the United States (Las Vegas) and finally, after twenty years, returned to Italy, where they now own a restaurant on the Amalfi coast. Growing up in the United States, she said her mother juggled, tamed lions (until she decided that menstrual blood was dangerous in that line of work), and tossed people back and forth with her feet for a living. She never learned English, and instead of reading her children bedtime stories she would lie on her back and juggle the kids with her feet. The caller said she would like to write about her family but is more interested in a book about Hebrew women at the time of Christ. I smell a Christian theme not to my liking or style. When you've got that sort of family in your kit bag, why on earth would you want to write about anything else?

Walking into Ellen's house last night, I felt depressed. The unreality of my situation seemed too hard to imagine living with—the absence of Mother, Christian, Eliza, Justin—and the liveliness of the Papoulakos house came down on me. "I think I will stop drinking," I told Ellen.

Later, sitting on the bleachers at a Patrick Henry High School football game, I had trouble catching the football spirit. But there were a couple of plays, when a lightning-fast kid grabbed the ball and cut through the players like a panther, that were thrilling. And the wide-eyed Papoulakos girls, their social antennae out as far as they could extend, were a visual delight. Like all the other perfectly groomed teenage girls at the game, they drifted like starlets around the bleachers, saying hello to their friends.

❧

Once again, I'm faced with the truth that I am not a sex object. A third man, hooked online, slipped away. I can't say I'm upset. He was a nice person but not interesting. What he thinks of me can be summed up in his silence since he left. I was interested when he said his ex-wife had warned him before marrying that she didn't love him and she wasn't a good bet for marriage. "She must have been quite something," I said, "for you to want to go ahead with it." He nodded. "She was a very electric personality, made everything fun, knew everybody, and was a sharp dresser." There it is.

We await the storm that may be a hurricane. Somewhere in North Carolina, Isabel is a giant pinwheel churning her way north. Our poor waterlogged trees will have a hard time holding firm.

THE NEXT DAY

The Artiglias' dead tree fell on my new writer's cottage. I returned to my house after Hurricane Isabel (I had stayed the night at the Papoulakos') to find such devastation that I was beyond feeling anything. Two giant trees lay across the yard, with a third having crushed the roof of my brand-new cottage. I was the worst hit of anyone in town. But my mother's painting on glass survived, my book of Auden poems is dry, and *all* the furniture—*all*—is undamaged. Every picture, plant, rug, chair, and pillow was spared. But after seeing how fragile a house is, now that a tree has demolished mine, I cannot look at any house as all that secure.

The town does what it always does in a crisis—pays attention. Offers of help from people I barely knew came in. Justin arrived from New York and has been my strong arm, with a chain saw attached, ever since. All over town, men in pickup trucks with chain saws were driving around, looking happier than I'd seen them in a long time.

How primitive one becomes without electricity. Without hot water, life immediately becomes difficult and dirty. And by seven o'clock in the evening all activity grinds to a halt. Two nights ago, sitting in a dark living room, all that was left to do, had I chosen it, was to play the piano, perhaps compose a new song. People become more precious and essential.

Shortly before Hurricane Isabel struck, I received an e-mail from a Match.com subscriber saying that he had just found me online and that apparently we lived in the same town. He said he found my description "quite interesting" although he had to be honest and tell me he was "a Republican and not an intellectual."

I wrote him back and thanked him for his interest and honesty but admitted that his views gave me pause. "They may not be red flags," I said, "but they're certainly pink. Truthfully, I'm not even a Democrat, but more a Socialist looking for a leader. And I have a very active life of the mind."

He wrote back and said that maybe we weren't a good match but he thought I sounded very interesting and how about just having dinner. To which I replied, "Well, I guess that would be okay. The last man I was seriously interested in didn't even believe in Social Security."

We made plans to meet that were canceled by the hurricane but a few days later we rescheduled.

Tonight, Ragan Phillips comes for a date. I cannot say I'm feeling wildly attractive. Sixty-four is sixty-four. What one loves is inside.

◦◦◦

Ragan Phillips, tall, bubbly, and smart, sixty-seven, from a small town in Kentucky, has come into my life. And he lives in Ashland! He comes with three grandchildren and a chocolate Lab puppy. Last night we had dinner at the Ironhorse, and tonight he will come by before I leave for Italy. I think he would be easy to love. He is "open to the new," as Mother would say. I am struck by how he resembles J in certain ways. He is confident, manly, and sexy. He is not put off by our political differences, and he is a risk taker, someone who thinks about what could be if only. . . . This last is not like J, who almost always played it safe.

◦◦◦

Yesterday, dear Ragan brought me a guidebook of Tuscany and a bottle of Chanel perfume for my trip. He looks older in the daylight, but so, I'm bound to admit, do I.

◦◦◦

IN ITALY

An exuberant e-mail from Ragan. He is still interested and open and full of life. The desire to love someone in an easy, growing way has been awakened. But I don't want to confuse him with a lovable dog. That being said, I was so cheered to hear from him. It is hard not to hope.

Just now I am sitting in the *biblioteca* on Via della Sapienza in Siena at a library table with three young students all poring over their books. The quiet is barely broken by the turning of a page or the hum of a distant heater. The walls are lined with ancient hide-covered books behind mesh-covered doors.

I despair of ever really learning Italian. The prepositions get me down, no pun intended. Articles escape me and other languages, learned earlier, bump me off the track. "Your Italian was better when I first knew you," remarked Jennifer. *Quindi, quale, oh my golly!* A baby would understand more. If I was here long enough, I would crack the code.

While working on a self-portrait [part of an art class I arranged for the writers at Spannocchia] I was brought to tears by my own face as I stared at it in a mirror. How old I am! It was hard to bear. Jennifer spoke of a similar experience she had when she was part of a class, where she was asked to stand in front of a mirror and look at herself without any clothes on for ten uninterrupted minutes. "I found myself crying, not only because I was no longer young but I could see the hurts and bruises and sorrow—the way I sometimes see them in others—and I was filled with compassion."

To be able to feel compassion for oneself and not, as I felt, aversion and disgust, is the sign of a humble heart, and Jennifer has one.

❧

One of the young American interns at Spannocchia told me this story.

Originally, her family came from Italy. There were three brothers, whose parents died. The two oldest brothers decide to go to America, and they ask a friend of the family to keep the youngest until they can afford to send for him.

When the two older brothers go down to the emigration office to buy their tickets, they get separated. Both say they want to go to America, but which America, North or South? asks the official. They don't know the difference. One says "America" again and his passport is stamped NORTH AMERICA. The other says "the same as my brother," but since the brother can't be found, the official stamps SOUTH AMERICA on his passport.

The two brothers board separate ships and are lost to each other. Meanwhile, the third brother's keeper secretly wants him to marry her daughter when he is grown, so she tells him his brothers have abandoned him, and after duly marrying the woman's daughter and having a family he dies, thinking the story was true.

Sometime later, one of his daughters discovers a box belonging to her grandmother, containing letters from the two older brothers. The descendents of one brother live in Argentina, the other in Boston. The grandson in Italy is a wealthy man, and he flies the impoverished Argentinean relatives to Italy, where they are joined by the other brother's relatives from Massachusetts. Today the family is together again.

Lost and Found. Every family could tell its own tale.

∾

Home, home, home! The dearness of my house, town, and friends sweeps over me like a familiar language. Since returning I have filled my ears with overdue news from my children and friends. I am grateful for my safe return.

Yesterday's energy session with Peggy was a complete blessing. I got off the table feeling entirely restored, all the jet lag gone. I felt grounded, vital, back. My fears of losing my mental capacities and my eyesight were lifted. "I'm afraid of losing my marbles," I confessed. "I put all your marbles back," she said.

For twenty days I have been without a Chinese journal in which to write. During those "lost days" I was smitten by a man who lives in Ashland. Now, unsmitten, I sit here wondering whether I am past marrying or partnering. He went from being a tall handsome man with a distinctive voice to a huge blow-up plastic figure with a booming voice. I felt as if I had no room to move.

The gulf between us kept widening in my mind until I felt dizzy with the difference. What I've discovered is how much space around me I need—to sit, to talk, to think, to be. Ragan, on the other hand, seems to be happier on the move. I have been almost overwhelmed by movement: errands, taking drives to man-made lakes that leave me cold. I was relieved when he announced he was going home last night. "I don't want to push a good thing," he said. I thanked him.

I am amazed at how much time I need to collect myself to feel whole. At this point, perhaps always, I would not feel comfortable with a man around all the time.

∽

Twenty-four hours later I have changed my mind again. Ragan's phone call, after the above had been written, brought the tide back in. We know each other a little better and have agreed to take our friendship a little slower. "Perhaps an engineer and a philosopher can't meet but I'm hoping they can," he said.

Lots of conversations afterward with others—Elizabeth, Pat, Debbie, Sarah. This is where women have such an advantage—this ability to connect with friends. Sarah made me laugh and think. She cautioned against looking at Ragan as a reflection of myself. "Narcissism! Think of him as a pine cone or a glass of Diet Coke, something that has dropped into your lap, or been given to you, but is distinct from you."

All my wiser friends advise me to take it easy, enjoy him for who he is.

∽

I'm still up in the air about Ragan. He seems awfully large sometimes, and my ability to let him be himself when it doesn't square with my self-image is marginal. I don't know if he can be deprogrammed. It would be cruel in a way. Who am I to change someone's whole life and conditioning? He would have to want it for himself.

∽

Early Saturday morning. I could not sleep. I missed my evening call with Ragan, who finally got through after I'd gone to bed. This morning I thought how similar loving is to building a fire. It goes out if left untended. Reading Robert Ellsberg's chapter on "Learning to Love," I thought of how real love opens doors to something larger than oneself.

Ragan continues to unfold like fabric that gets more beautiful with each flip of the bolt. I love the way he alternates so easily between understanding and silliness. I can feel my heart growing daily, which has its uncomfortable aspects, as if it could fall with the weight of love and break.

I leave for California tomorrow. The last hour with Ragan in my living room was a confirmation of his worth. He spoke his mind about his heart and it was then that I wanted to sit at his feet (as in fact I did) and hold his hand in mine.

Here are my deepest thoughts. When the tide of love is in, I swim happily on the surface, free to go in any direction while floating. When the tide is out, I can see what has been hidden by the water, the old boots and cast-off tires the water has obscured.

I am also aware of how important it is to think about one's life as a story. Introducing a major character at the last minute can either unbalance or reinforce the plot. The idea of a beloved companion to share my life could become a dissonant chord that ruins the symphony. And what about Ragan's life and story? Would I be what *he* needs?

Liftoff day for California. Wanting to be there competes with wanting to be here. Who could turn away from a man who puts you on a monthly subscription to Peet's Coffee, sends his yardman around to clean the gutters, and knows how to talk about real things on the phone? Pat and Debbie already have us married.

En route to California. Below me in the late afternoon sun the land looks like the frozen floor of an ocean, which it probably was. The surface has the pink opalescent shine of an abalone shell. Now the sun has sunk a little. The empty snow-covered ridges that are sweeping ahead into the Rockies always amaze me. Water must have raked over these mountains for thousands of years. Below is a thick blanket of cloud that moves under us in the opposite direction. Now I see what may be part of the Sierra—the buttes are steeper, canyons more pronounced. I imagine whales swimming between the mountains, skimming down the flanks to the bottom. The same snake-shaped river continues to move west. The path of least resistance is beautiful. As the sky is drained of color, the mountains look like giant algae leaves, veined and wrinkled. I cannot see any signs of light or life, other than an occasional straight-line road. So many centuries and immigrations later, we still have not come close to filling this country up.

All day yesterday I blinked away with my eyes, taking "pictures"—the mist over Monterey as I came over the hill from Carmel, my granddaughter Rhys's smile, her brother Toby's earnest face with the basketball under his chin, Eliza's smile, Christian Jr.'s bright blue eyes.

Last night in Jim and Belinda's house with the blazing fire and lighted Christmas tree, with Francesca Farr and John

Hicks, was close to heaven. Here were souls of such quality and shine. I want Ragan to know them. We found ourselves singing or reading favorite hymns, Hymn 289 and another that John read aloud from one of Belinda's hymnals. Later, at the restaurant, Jim made friends with everyone on either side, confessed that perhaps he wasn't really a Republican. But what a strong fine mind he has. I don't really want him to switch parties, or there'd be nothing for me to push up against. John looks more refined, handsomer than ever. That small sad-eyed man with nut-brown skin and little hands is quiet with grief over Priscilla, now over two years gone. But he is content to be so. Belinda's eighty-four-year-old sister died earlier this month. All this we exchanged over our meal.

Yesterday morning on the Carmel beach with the bright sun and mist, I thanked God for my eyes that I could see the glory of it in every detail. Joy wakes me up at an earlier hour, makes me sleepless and more alive.

A wonderful talk with Ragan. I found myself trying to limit our conversational exposure because I was afraid he would say something that would sow doubt in my heart. His daughter Meg surprised him with a visit from his younger daughter, Kellady, and his dog, Bear, which she had been keeping for him. He had not expected either of them. He misses me. "Last night I reached for you," he said, and I could tell he was in tears. Part of me was moved; part of me wanted to say, "Get a grip."

It is early Christmas morning and I have already spoken to Ragan. I love him, but not with the passionate intensity I have loved other men. "This is not my usual story," I told him.

There is a stage in the formation of a paper-white narcissus when the flower is still encased in the shaft but pressing against it, visible in the skin, waiting to burst into the air. That is how I feel about Ragan. I am still shy, not wanting to be observed by others in this stage.

On my last day in California, Ragan reads me a story over the phone he wrote about a woman who is going to break off a relationship but goes to Italy and decides she loves him after all. At one point, he chokes up. I was so touched by the thought and appalled at the writing that I didn't know what to say. "It's really a love letter to you," he said. My feelings have been painfully full, balancing between wanting to rush forward in a reckless way and worrying that loving someone this much could hurt me terribly if he pulled away.

In the air. Going home. A bright blue sky, favorable tailwinds and a smooth ride. Ragan's love has been so constant and caring that I am beginning to feel my balance—acquired after years of walking without a partner—deserting me. I am as clear as one can be in this high blaze that committing myself to Ragan is committing myself to him for the rest of my life.

Rereading *Einstein's Dreams* by Alan Lightman reminds me of how we shape our lives like a story, how unconsciously we attract plots, outcomes, and other characters who undermine or complicate our unfolding drama. We supply the meaning—and therein lies the difference between one life and another.

2004

January 1

Home again. An ecstatic Ragan at the airport, an ecstatic me. A New Year's Eve as loving as I had hoped for, and on New Year's Day we were together. How I feel right now I am not sure. But after forty-eight hours with Ragan telling me in no uncertain terms how much in love with me he is, I begin to feel crowded again, as if I cannot be so far in the lead. In another way, it is Ragan who leads me, willing to let me take my time as my feelings grow. "I'm glad you waited for me to catch up," I said to him. "You'll never catch up," he answered. This is romantic stuff—to have, at the age of sixty-four, a man who is passionate about you.

Not even two days after being together, I am beginning to feel "on overwhelm," as Mother would say. I feel too full of doubt about my abilities to enjoy him on enough levels to make a go of it. It upsets me to realize how far the pendulum can swing, but I can't deny that the peace and quiet I feel at this very moment is as delicious as any of the idylls we've had in recent days.

Yesterday at Peggy's we talked about men. I told her my journal was ecstatic one day, despairing the next. She said her journals have looked like that for twenty-seven years. She counseled me to be patient, to learn to flow more easily between the physical, emotional, and spiritual aspects of my life. If my mother had been looking for someone to send me, she would have wanted it to be someone like Ragan, with a big heart. "The other things would not have mattered."

That being said, I don't think it's wise to resist my doubts any more than I resist my enthusiasms. Eliza's remark about Ragan's place in my life rings true: "You have spent a lot of energy, consciously and unconsciously, making it all right to be alone, and before that you had a traumatic relationship, so it's not easy to change." I thought that was brilliant and, coming from one of my own children, touching.

A coat of snow fell on the town last night. I walked around the neighborhood. There is such a charm and familiarity to it, each house holding its souls inside like candles quietly burning.

An old book [*The Choice Is Always Ours*] just surfaced in an upstairs bookcase, like a bright stone that had sunk into the mud. The editors write of the false gods of success, happiness, peace, and security. The first is obvious. The last three have worked their way into my bones.

Yesterday I felt vaguely disoriented. I wondered if it lay in my concerns about my relationship with Ragan. I want to put a cork in his bottle, keep his feelings more contained so I can handle them better, have room for my own. He is such a good man and I miss him, while worrying that he may not give me enough room to be myself. We are not that different from animals in a zoo. Each needs to have some private territory, enough space to be restored.

Ragan home from a business trip! He mounted the stairs yesterday afternoon and was such balm for my eyes and heart. We stood for at least fifteen minutes with our arms around each other. I wonder about this love I feel. When he gives me stuffed animals from Disney World it makes me feel it's wrong. But there is something more elemental about him that thrills me. My heart is eased when he is here. His presence in my house comforts me. From one visit to the next his things accumulate: a jacket in the hall closet, shaving gear upstairs, now a Range Rover outside.

A serious staph infection put Ragan into the hospital for three nights, where I slept on the floor by his bed. The worst is now over. Ragan had a good afternoon and evening. This morning he is strong-voiced and happy. I slept at home and needed every minute in my bed. Now, back in my wing chair with the sun streaming through the shutters, I am full of quiet peace and gratitude.

In the years from sixty to seventy, my mother used to say often, are a wonderful decade. The chaos of career and child rearing is finished. Your children are companions. Friends are still, for the most part, alive and well. And there is a kind of creative contentment that runs through one's days that is like no other time in life. The tide is in and the richness of the ocean is all around. But Ragan's hospital stay gave me a look into the future. We are not young. One of us will be caring for the other, putting aside the joys of sex for the joys of service.

As we marked time in the hospital, we had long talks about our relationship that filled me with doubt again. To be such a person of the word, who thrives on its use and pronunciation, makes it hard to listen to Ragan, who speaks so fast that often I cannot hear the endings of his sentences. They have butter-knife edges.

That being said, we also have discussions that are deeply satisfying, where I don't feel the differences. I worry that I am fighting off a clarity I don't want because it might force me to end the relationship. And I am really appalled at the paucity of men's relationships, the way they do not trust other men except when they are working as a team. Could this be why war is so intoxicating? Could this be why, when a job is over, the friendships men form dissolve so quickly, whereas with women the job is how and where we met, not why.

I must write this down: The fire has gone out. Flipping back in my journal to less than a month ago, you'd think that I was writing about a different man. What is wrong with me?

Most people, consciously or not, have a list of what they want in a partner. With Ragan, most of the big-ticket items on my list were checked off: scrupulously honest, generous, full of life, deep capacity and desire to love. But he was a Republican, educated at the U.S. Naval Academy, which was about as far removed from the philosophically saturated, small Catholic women's college I attended as possible. He wasn't particularly at home in what he called my "highly literate world." As for conversation, he wasn't against it, but he got lost quickly in the analytical thickets at my end of the exchange. Conversely, my brain wanted to explode when he tried to explain the simplest mathematical formulas, or tell me how energy was created by—I can't even complete this sentence without revealing my inability to follow his explanation.

Up very early, yet I am glad for the additional hours. Ragan is probably going to be leaving my life. I have great respect and affection for him, but his needs for me are too strong.

It seems to me that many women, if not most, get to a certain age and want to get out from under the marital responsibilities that a husband necessarily imposes. So why would I be looking to assume them? My life is not lonely. It has a high degree of freedom and independence. A sexual life, while nourishing, is not essential. Independence *is* essential, even for women friends. My relationship with Francesca, for example, works because I do not rely on her for my life or entertainment. We are both free.

Nina Peace, a great soul in our town, died at fifty-three last night of a heart attack. The community is stunned. Amy, at Vintage Auto, wept in my arms when I ran into her at the bank. "She helped so many people," she said. That is what everyone who knew her said upon hearing the terrible news.

This evening, reading about William Blake, I find this poem by him that fits her:

> *Seek Love in the pity of others' woe,*
> *In the gentle relief of another's care,*
> *In the darkness of night and the winter's snow,*
> *With the naked and outcast—See love there.*

Several years before she died, Nina copied down the words below, by the writer Barry Lopez, and put them in a frame for our mutual friend, Pat:

In our best moments we remember to ask ourselves what it is we are doing, whom we are benefitting by these acts. One of the great dreams of mankind must be to find someplace between the extremes of nature and civilization where it is possible to live without regret.

Living in a small town keeps the facts of life, that we are bound for the grave, squarely in front of you. Nina Peace's funeral yesterday with her son, mother, and husband walking down the aisle behind her casket, confirmed this. I realized how much I love the people here, how much my story has woven itself into the stories of everyone in town.

One of those stories revolves around young Elizabeth Papoulakos, who burst into the house a few days ago to talk about her broken heart. She sat across from me, so young and elastic, like the curls that bounced on her shoulders. She is a slender flower, perfumed with whatever the latest body gel is, glowing with natural vitality, but her heart is breaking as she tries to imagine life without her boyfriend.

ๆ๏

It occurs to me that we all have our keyhole on life. The size and shape of the keyhole determines how we view everything.

Reading a book by John Howard Griffin, *Scattered Shadows,* on going blind, is like food for me. After his sight was destroyed, he entered into a deeper, more spiritually intense life.

Blindness was a revelation because it exposed the enormous ability we have to be distracted by the things of this world, and the fundamental deficiencies of a strictly academic education. Being sightless demanded that I learn from experience in the most primal, clarifying manner.

Before he went blind, he tells the story of not having enough money to pay for lodging in Paris before his train departed. So he spent the night on the stone floor of a stairwell.

Instead of immersing it in myself, I was immersing myself in it. All I had done was change my attitude. I was still miserable, but it had become unimportant. I had ceased to be a person judging everything on the basis of pleasure or comfort. I had gone out of myself to the value of things in themselves, and I have never since been able to step back consistently into mere self-interest. This is the crucial difference, I believe, between the person whose life is monotonous and the one who is adventure-prone.

After Griffin's sight began to deteriotate, a Benedictine priest who is blind counsels him:

Your main task will be to persevere. Remember always that word. Your main temptations will be against perseverance. . . . Sometimes our deepest wound comes from hurt pride in this, because we think we do not have some great gift to offer God and the world. But the important thing, in God's eyes, is not what we have to give, but that we hold nothing back, that we refuse to give God even our wretchedness, our stubbornness, our littleness of soul. Sometimes these are the only things we've got, eh?

As Griffin demonstrated, he was never without supporting players who entered the stage with great precision as other players took their leave. Even the order of their appearance had an evolutionary sequence: the blind beggar, then the poet, then the monk. Each built upon the one before.

As we drove home from dinner last night, Ragan said, "I read somewhere that a relationship is over when one of the people starts paying the other back for favors." He was referring to the check for $30 I had given him this morning to reimburse him for some books he had paid for. I protested but added "I'm not saying the relationship isn't over, but the check has nothing to do with it."

By the time we pulled up outside my house, the truth was clear. All the reasons I do love him were exhibited; his manliness, his love of me, his forthright honesty, his ability to feel. Yet he himself had nailed it in his last letter: the stimulation I need is not there. "You're quite a woman, Phyllis. As they say in baseball, you can play all the positions." I've never had a better compliment. "Right now," he continued, "it's *man overboard*. For a while I'll be near the mother ship, but in time it will be too late to get back. I'll have drifted too far away." He did not say this hopefully, only realistically. As he himself said, "All the pieces of the puzzle were not there."

That night, as I watched him stride purposefully across the lawn in the dark to his car, I felt relief mixed with misgiving and then more relief. This was a wonderful man, but there were too many differences between us. By ending the relationship, I had dodged the bullet for both of us.

∾

I am reading Karen Armstrong's *The Spiral Staircase,* where she talks about her seizures and how, like Tennyson and Bosch, they made her aware of the darkness "beneath the happy surface of things." I see how pushing the darkness away can wind up obscuring deeper levels of perception. I do it instinctively all the time.

∾

The book party for Ellen Goodman in Washington was a little hard on my ego. All the media lights—like Daniel Schorr, Nina Totenberg, Tom Oliphant, and Linda Wertheimer—were there, looking right past me. I felt pretty small and insignificant, as if I had already died.

There's nothing like a Washington power party to trigger a person's insecurities, make you feel like the unpopular kid at recess. But I remember one afternoon soiree, when I lived in Washington, held at the French ambassador's house, on Kalorama Road, which reminded me of what everybody, powerful or not, really wants.

It was, ostensibly, a party for children who later were going on to the circus. But there were a lot of stock adult characters hanging around the hors d'oeuvres—elegant women wearing the self-aware expressions of faces that had been too much photographed, little circles of people clustered around the presently powerful. A tall, flawlessly dressed man in his midforties, with a bright red tie flung like a flag against his chest, strode into the dining room like a lord. "How arrogant he acts," whispered my friend Alice. "I guess he hasn't been indicted yet," I whispered back. Pre-Indictment Man is a distinct species in Washington.

My ticket to this embassy party was Emily, a ten-year-old neighbor with Down syndrome who sometimes came over to my house to "play Dorfee" (Dorothy in The Wizard of Oz*), which involved trying on all my shoes to see which ones made the best sound when she clicked the heels together. Emily took one look at the center table laden with éclairs, cookies, and punch and knew just what to do. For the next half hour she worked the table like a pro, resting quietly on a side chair between courses. Finally, I decided it was time to interrupt the grazing cycle.*

"Come on, Em, let's go socialize. That's what you're supposed to do at a party."

"Okay," said Emily.

I spotted a young mother and daughter across the room and headed toward them.

"Hi," I said. "We'd like to practice socializing. Can we socialize with you?"

The woman looked down at Emily and smiled. "Sure." She extended her hand. "Hi, what's your name?"

"Emily," she said. Then there was silence.

"Now, Em," I coached, "you must ask her a question back."

Emily thought a moment, pushed her glasses up the bridge of her nose, and looked up into the woman's face. "Do you like me?"

The woman looked startled and then amused. I gave Emily a hug. "That's a great question, Emily, the one everyone else in the room is too afraid to ask."

It strongly occurs to me that I am happier alone. This doesn't mean I'm on my own. Far-flung and near-at-hand friends support me, give me meaning and understanding. But as Nikki said last night, at our age we want to be free. There is an exhilaration about it that expands one's possibilities. Being partnered tethers you, and only a great love, such as I had for my mother or have for my children, enables you to endure it, make it bear fruit.

I am unusually aware of time's passage. My friend Elizabeth, despite her on-going vitality at eighty, seems smaller, less indomitable; another close friend, Pat, is suffering from a leg that cannot support her. How fast we move across the stage. Thornton Wilder is so right. We don't stay at the dinner table very long.

Last night, I missed the people who give me strength. Actually it was only one person, Mother. Coming down the stairs, I felt the emptiness on the ground floor, of my house and my life.

A Sunday alone. A few hours cleaning up the cottage and feeling the loss of Ragan—increasingly, as the days go by. It is an emotional and physical loss, and I know that it is not enough to make a cake. But it sneaks up on me when I see Gerry put his hand on Neale's knee, or I slip into bed and remember the solid comfort of having Ragan beside me. So I am paying a price after all, which only seems fair.

Today I went to Charlottesville to hear Dr. Paul Farmer, the subject of Tracy Kidder's book, *Men to Match My Mountains,* give a talk about his hospital and work in Haiti. I found myself put off by the people in the room. They were so drab and uninteresting looking, so nunlike and Catholic, reminding me of all the county-wide Catholic Action meetings I went to during high school, all those mimeographed sheets of bad songs and unkindled prose. But I was put in my place when, one by one, they spoke. How brilliantly colored and interesting they all were as soon as they opened their mouths! Human beings are always so much richer on the inside. An affection for each person grew inside me when he or she began to speak.

Lord, let me not be a complete creature of habit. Is there even a minute during my waking hours when I am not gratifying myself in some predictable way: toast, coffee, nap, book, telephone, bath? A thought I've expressed but not written down: Ashland is a good place to live if I am doing serious work because it does not distract me. But if I am living on the surface, going from one piece of toast to another, it is a wasteland.

Karen Armstrong's book is so astonishingly apt, like the answer to the question and reproach at the center of my life. Here, or rather *there,* she is, a person unknown to me who is working away at her loom of words on my behalf, without knowing it. Her thoughts are the light I have needed to hold over my own conditioned mind to dissolve the threads that bind it.

When I was working in television, the phone rang constantly. I had to go to endless meetings to discuss shooting schedules and talk for hours at a time with colleagues about concept. But now . . . the telephone rarely rang, and I would sometimes go for two or three days at a time without speaking to anybody. I was alone with my books. . . .

At first this silence had seemed a deprivation, a symbol of an unwanted isolation. I had resented the solitude of my life and fought it. But gradually the enveloping quiet became a positive element, almost a presence, which settled comfortably and caressingly around me like a soft shawl. . . . I discovered that I felt at home in the silence, which compelled me to enter my interior world and walk around there. Without the distraction of constant conversation, the words on the page began to speak directly to my inner self. . . . Silence itself had become my teacher. —Karen Armstrong, The Spiral Staircase

My feelings and thoughts have centered themselves on Ragan, who brought so much easy intimacy into my life. My head knows that my emotions are too strong to reason with. If he were here it would be hard to resist the pull of his arms and his tenderness, even though once my emotional needs are met my more demanding judgmental intellect wants to be fed as well, and this he cannot do. There is no recourse but to withdraw.

Again, Karen Armstrong:

The silence in which I live has also opened up my ears and eyes to the suffering of the world. In silence, you begin to hear the note of pain that informs so much of the anger and posturing that pervade social and political life. Solitude is also a teacher. It is lonely; living without intimacy and affection tears holes in you. Saint Augustine . . . said somewhere that yearning makes the heart deep. It also makes you vulnerable.

The gift of Karen Armstrong's book during this first week of really sinking into my mother's life and letters (how closely those two used to be joined) is immeasurable. She leads my life, validates its worth, knows the cost, and understands the perils and rewards. She could not be a better companion.

Yesterday, after spending it transcribing the letters from Mother I'd saved, I realized there was a hole where all her letters from her year in France in 1985 should be. I went back upstairs into my closet and found a thick file labeled MOM'S LETTERS, which doubles the amount of material I have to work with. I am finding what I need in abundance.

Missing in the above is my longing for Ragan, all the while distrusting it. Today in particular I have felt his absence sorely in the pit of my stomach, my arms, and my hands. It occurs to me that perhaps there has been a transfer of pain, that as I am feeling worse he is feeling better. This thought cheered me up and made me realize that I truly do care for him and always will. I just wish it were possible to come to a conclusion, the way one can when examining someone's DNA or blood, that a person is right or wrong for you. Yet my ambivalence is, I think, false in the main. I miss him, yes. But nothing essential has changed, nor should it. He is fine the way he is, more than fine. But right now I am feeling the words that Karen Armstrong wrote: *living without intimacy tears holes in you*. If it is the right, true thing to do, I am willing to be torn. But right now what, humanly, I want to do is call him, hear his voice, feel his love. But I will not. It would not be fair.

Beverly Nichols's book (*Merry Hall*), about his garden is responsible for my purchasing two crab apple trees and a Yoshino cherry.

An e-mail, finally, from Ragan last night. He was waiting for a letter from me. My head is empty this morning. The tide is out in every way.

I think I have gotten on the other side of longing.

I spent the day with more of Mother's letters. In the process of tracking down her life, I caught glimpses of my own and felt ordered by the simple act of slipping letters into chronological order and seeing a story line emerge.

❧

Yesterday morning I found a large pot of yellow flowers and a CD of Mozart piano sonatas on my front porch with a note from Ragan wishing me a happy Easter. The first thing I felt was relief, that he hadn't left me a long letter of the heart. The second thing I felt was criticism of *my* heart, which has cooled so quickly. He really is a gentleman in both senses of that word and I can find no fault in him, other than that we are incompatible.

❧

Another shock to the town: Jay Pace, longtime owner/editor of our local newspaper, has died of a cerebral hemorrhage! Like Nina, he lived a crowded, intense life. Like Nina, he was only in his fifties. Like Nina, he was a pillar of the community.

Death energizes the community, brings us together like survivors in a plot we will one day be written out of. At Jay's funeral reception yesterday, it took almost two hours to get from the back of the line to the front. Everyone in town was there—the police chief, the mailman, and hundreds of others, including several Episcopal bishops. The room rang with a kind of exhilaration that may be partly the relief of being passed over. But I think it was also the delight of being together and paying tribute to Jay.

A funeral in a small town is intense. The one for Jay at Saint James the Less was jam-packed, not a space available that wasn't filled. I took the last chair in the balcony. Jay's singing group gave us "Peace Like a River" and "On the Banks of the Jordan," which they had vowed to sing for each other at their funerals. Ira Andrews's rich voice, like warm delta mud, ran beneath the others. Chris Pace's eulogy to his father was full of jokes about his graduating in five years from college, his love of sports, and his hatred of players who didn't stick with the team that brought them. The sound of five hundred people laughing is a beautiful sound. But it was Steve Pace, the smaller and quieter younger brother, who brought the church to tears. At the end of his eulogy he asked the congregation to help him do something. "Close your eyes and think of Jay as you want to remember him"—I thought of him at the variety show at the piano—and then Steve sang, "Somewhere Over the Rainbow," Jay's favorite song.

It was such a loving, courageous act, by a deeply introverted man whose voice was not large but true. Toward the end, the congregation gently hummed along with him, unable to resist. This morning upon waking it did not seem possible that Jay was not waking up, too.

The town is going to stumble around for a while without him. I resolved to be a better person.

Must note that I saw Ragan yesterday morning on my walk. It was the annual Railroad Run, and he was standing behind the Hanover Arts and Activities building. He looked so handsome, his eyes were steady and loving, and when we parted he kissed me on the cheek. All day it stayed with me—a longing to be in the presence of such affection—and I wished I had not exposed myself to it. But a month has gone by and perhaps from his perspective it is time to meet normally as friends.

Seeing Ragan has unsettled me, physically and emotionally. This is not his fault. Even so, I noticed that his nose was running a little. These kinds of critiques would only get worse if we were together. But right now I am missing what was wonderful about him and forgetting what was not.

❦

Spring has arrived in full force. The tree we planted at Mom's memorial service is full of little leaf buds. The grass is juicy and shining. The dogwood outside my bedroom window is a floating white spray of flowers. I want to be outside to let the sun nourish my poor winter skin.

When I think about who around me holds me up, gives me meaning the way a mother can, it surprises me to realize that there is no one. Yet I move through the day without feeling any particular disorientation. The absence of landfall does not make me lose my bearings. I wonder whether I am truly detached and at peace, or if it is a loss of feeling.

A note from Ragan, asking for a chance to reexamine our relationship. I answered with a note saying that I am not yet over it and cannot risk being emotionally derailed.

❦

A solitary weekend, spent mostly in the garden. Physical and imaginative work go together. But the creative urge can be sabotaged by smaller urges to eat, sleep, or create something on a lower level, getting the easy reward of a shiny counter or a row of dinner napkins drying on a clothesline.

❦

This morning I went bird-watching with my friend Gerry, who came over with an extra pair of binoculars for me. I was amazed at his ability to separate one birdsong from another and to identify them so easily as they flew by. I came across what may have been a woodpecker half hidden by leaves. He had a white crown, streaked with red and black, a snowy breast, and gray feathers. Then, when I took my eyes from the binoculars, he disappeared, like a glimpse of truth that had slipped away.

I worked all day transcribing the last of Mom's letters. Then I began to slip mine between them. I found a letter from Dad written in 1980, recounting his whole recent life with his girl-friend and how badly it had ended, and how much he wanted to rebuild the family. The letters are allowing me, in a collected state, to experience what I wasn't open to or able to experience fully at the time.

Around two-thirty I got up for a break from the tidal wave of paper records—some of it quite powerful—but the simplicity of my original idea, to write a book about Mom, has been blurred by all the other people in my life, particularly the men who wanted in or out of it. Suddenly it's about me. The notebook binders, divided by years, are becoming loaded down with data that only tell me one important thing—that life goes at a heartbreaking breakneck speed, even as we sit quietly in a chair and chafe at our inactivity.

I rode my bicycle over to [sculptor] Jerry Peart's house to sit behind his barn and talk about art. We both agreed that the only thing worse than reporting to oneself would be reporting to someone else, although he wishes that someone would tell him what to do. "I am capable of doing whatever I want," he said, "but getting the vision of what I want is what's difficult."

❧

Today I threw three huge plastic bags of old letters in the trash. They are the last of my harvest, an attempt to separate the wheat from the chaff. I have tossed out all fan letters, saved all letters to and from my children, and reserved the letters written by or sent to my ex-husband and documents pertaining to the divorce, unsure as to how or whether they can be useful in a larger sense. In addition, I've tried to hang on to certain letters that shed an unflattering but truthful light upon me. I am, I believe, finally able to look at myself dispassionately.

Reading old letters from friends who have drifted away brings them right back to me, fresh and ready to relate to again. I am tempted to pick up the phone and renew the relationship, like a library book.

As my capacity to retain information shrinks, it is reassuring to be able to know, because of what I have saved, when things of importance happened. A plasticized holy card from the funeral of Christian's son Matthew tells me that he died on May 15, 1994—ten years ago. What a day of sorrow that was! A letter from Jay Pace, dead less than six weeks, thanks me for Wilfred Sheed's essay on suffering and tells me about his own spiritual practice, which includes reading a page a day from Julian of Norwich. My letters are a paper empire, a documented version of what swims in my head, minus the terrible pain that often accompanied my life at the time.

If we look upon our experiences as assets, we must manage to preserve or transfer those assets to other people before we die or they dissolve in the grave with us.

∾

Last night I hopped on my bike and rode down to Cross Brothers for a "wonder chicken" for my supper. The soft spring air was filled with the scent of grass clippings, moist earth, and flowering shrubs all mixed together. Riding down the street, I moved through bands of perfume.

On a whim I decided to stop by Dolo Kerr's on Center Street, and the two of us sat on her front porch and swapped news, gossip, and ideas. There is something so open-minded and easy about Dolo. She had heard I was in love. Her daughter told her that Ragan was a catch. I laughed. "He is, but I'm not." Dolo's face is like W. H. Auden's, a series of dried riverbeds with two bright blue pools for eyes that organize the whole.

Recently, when talking to my friend Nikki about face lifts, I implored her to resist. Looking at a friend who has had a face lift is like reading a book with half the pages ripped out.

∾

Yesterday I helped Ellen harvest her field full of peonies. While filling buckets full of flowers, her teenage daughter Laura came to join us. "I'm lonely," she said. There is an endlessness to young loneliness. You feel the emptiness of your life, so unfurnished, so bare of anything but dreams that may not come to pass. As we picked peonies side by side, I felt this sadness and tried to remember the poem by Gerard Manley Hopkins that addressed it:

> *Margaret are you grieving*
> *Over Goldengrove unleaving...*
> *It is the blight man was born for,*
> *It is Margaret you mourn for.*

Dinner last night with the new rector of a church in Ashland. How perverse is the heart. He mentioned his favorite book, *The Leopard,* which is also mine, and his favorite Mozart piano concerto, No. 27 (mine as well), and was, in many ways, what Ragan isn't. But there was no chemistry, just a pleasant evening with a pleasant man.

Lunch in New York with a radiant ninety-two-year-old Margot Wilkie, who personifies what Freya Stark wrote about getting old.

On the whole, age comes most gently to those who have some doorway into an abstract world—art, or philosophy, or learning—regions where the years are scarcely noticed and young and old can meet in a pale, truthful light.

I told her how well she looked. "Lots of makeup," she said, deflecting the praise.

Her Buddhist *rinpoche* and one of his students were upstairs in her apartment when she met me in the lobby. We spent most of our time talking about what we've learned in life. Margot recounted a long-ago evening with friends when her mother was still alive, discussing what love was without coming to a conclusion. The next morning she asked her mother how she would define it. "Love is understanding," she said. So, in this way, I think I do love Ragan, or at least my understanding of him creates the love I have.

The next day I had lunch with Gene Young. I found myself waxing eloquent on the subject of a friend's worth, hers in particular. I advanced the metaphor of a friend being like the net around a bag of onions that keeps the onions from rolling off the table.

A lost friend was returned this week. After years of estrangement, brought on by my thoughtless, hurtful response to her sister's death, Mary returned, as if nothing had ever gone wrong, her warm voice flowing into the phone. Her other sister, Nancy, must have held my place in the book. When a friend returns, an empire is restored.

New York in May is about as perfect a place to be as can be imagined. The leaves are squeaky clean and green, the air soft. Every street and face seems out of my reach: the gay homeboys in their pale pink shirts and caps, sweet-faced and doomed, the quivering intelligence of Swoosie Kurtz on stage, the joy of sitting in a room and listening to Justin read his lines for an upcoming audition. My heart begins to ache with the desire to live here and the knowledge that I can't.

In Washington, D.C.

Walking back from Starbucks on Connecticut Avenue this morning I stopped to look at a tree spangled with dew—each purple leaf covered with bright balls of light still holding their own against the sun, which will eventually burn them up. I did not work hard enough to find the precise words that would pick out the image on a page. Poets do that; they make us think they strolled past the tree and effortlessly found the words to describe it.

∾

An honest but empty day's work yesterday, trying to find a thread I could follow to begin my mother's book. But I am too close to the material I have amassed to see it, and my poor mother is drowned by other people's voices. The term "pilgrim soul," from a Yeats poem, popped out at me as a good description of her. There was something so steadfast about her.

Artistically, I don't find my own life compelling material—all those boyfriends, all that angst. It seems like the same script over and over again. Yet if there was a way to get beneath the surface and redeem it, make it stand for something more, I would. Perhaps I am too blind or proud to use what is there.

∾

Last night, my young friend Mary Boodell gave me a free ticket to the Richmond Symphony, where she is the first flutist. She is pregnant and as she sat on the stage with her flute, the crashing sounds of Mahler's Fifth Symphony swirled around her. I thought of her unborn baby curled like a small dinner roll in her womb, listening the way one might listen from beneath the water in a swimming pool. What an introduction to the world, to be growing in the middle of music, soothed and stimulated by it.

The French philosopher and mathematician, Blaise Pascal died at thirty-nine, a fully realized, deeply accomplished person. Today we mature so much more slowly. We are too time-driven, distracted, and diverted by trivia to pay attention to our growth. One of the aspects of Mom's life that I found so endearing was her inability to know what to do with herself. She spent a good deal of time wondering, as she phrased it, *how to put in my day.* I think that knowing how to put in your day is one of the great unspoken problems of being alive.

On May 30, Ragan came back into my life. The only person more surprised than I was Ragan, but when he stood outside my front door my heart melted. At dinner, he said he felt like a condemned felon. I pushed everything on the table away to hold his hands, and when he held mine I realized how much I had missed them—and him. Being as honest as I can, I have missed being loved by him, but, equally important, I have missed loving him. What this does to my reservations about our intellectual compatibility I don't know. But if we go slowly perhaps we will find out together. As Ragan wrote, "We're close," and that did not change even when apart. I care about what happens to him, more deeply than I knew. And once again I am on the verge of leaving for Italy. But knowing he is waiting for me to return is a reassuring bookend at the end of the trip.

In Italy at Villa Spannocchia with my friend Valerie, who decided to come along for the experience

A sleepless night. I wake up to a full moon in the window. The earth is fragrant with damp earth and cool summer air. Valerie wakes up, too, and we talk for an hour or more about our mothers. She also misses her mother, and she wept a little when she talked about her. All through the night an insistent bird just outside our window makes a one-note call every other second. It doesn't stop until close to dawn.

There is such a feeling of home here. Last night after dinner, I sat on a stone bench in front of the villa porch, looked into the star-filled sky and listened to the chatter of animals in the woods. It brought me great peace. I miss Ragan. The delight I feel is the delight of feeling a solid love replacing the quixotic one.

Venice! We came on a bright cool day with Pachelbel playing in the Opera House. It is difficult to say whether light or darkness becomes Venice more. Night or day, it is the most brilliantly beautiful place I have ever seen. But beauty costs! A glass of tonic water (no gin) costs $15 in the Piazza San Marco. A dinner in a small al fresco restaurant, $38; a half-hour gondola ride down the Rialto, $35. There is an absence of clatter and noise in Venice, as if all sound is absorbed by the thick stones of the houses, the water in the canals. Last night, coming back to our hotel, Valerie saw a rat scurry past the hotel's front door. Venice strikes me as a town *full* of rats, barely hidden from the tourists' view.

Florence charmed me all over again. A few hours by myself, walking, walking, my legs so strong from all the steps and hills I've climbed on this visit. A chorus of Italian men were singing "Blue Moon" on the loggia of the Uffizi, a Dante performance artist in gold body paint nearby.

I was surprised at how Assisi did *not* charm me. The punishing steepness of the streets, the lack of trees, and the dry bleached appearance of the houses had no appeal. The men of Assisi all reminded me of the paintings of Saint Francis. They are small and wiry with intense, thin faces, their hair cut stubble short, like tonsures. The people of Assisi are gentle, kindly people, as if the peacefulness of the saint had sunk into their collective unconscious. But Assisi itself, with that huge, money-making, tourist-attracting basilica dwarfing the rest of the town, left me cold.

Home. I arrive to find a basket of flowers hanging from my front door with a loving note from Ragan. He is always surprising me. I will never get used to it. I love the way he wants to take care of things, how he coils my hose, fixes my lawnmower, paves my way. These are not small considerations at any age, much less mine. Eliza said she wanted to cry when she heard I was back with Ragan. Justin said, "You've come to your senses."

Can this be love, this quiet, accepting affection I feel, coupled with a deepening concern and desire to be with this man? What a great undeserved gift to be loved in this way. Some kind of a sea change is occurring in me.

Ragan's two daughters are a real balm for Ragan. They are loving and intelligent women. Playing croquet on his lawn with the three grandsons, and Bear weaving an ecstatic circle around us all, was a wonderful gift.

As his confidence in my affection for him grows, Ragan becomes more himself. He wrote an epic poem, consisting of two words, *my* and *darling*. He laughed when I asked him to recite the "ninth stanza" again.

Rereading *Einstein's Dreams* by Alan Lightman reminds me of the way we shape our lives like a story, how unconsciously we attract plots, outcomes, and other characters who undermine or complicate our unfolding drama. We supply the meaning and therein lies the difference between one life and another.

A Monday of good intentions: exercise, diet, put money in the bank, redirect my boat toward a deeper part of the sea. There is a temptation to drift from the center of my life, to seek security in another relationship. I feel it with Ragan, with whom I am falling more deeply in love. Suddenly I want guarantees, outward signs, public pledges—i.e., marriage—and whereas once I worried that he'd ask me, now I worry that he won't. In my defense I think it is natural to desire permanence when it comes to love. At this time in my life it seems more meaningful to be married, particularly when there are children and grandchildren involved. I do love this man. He does what he promises. You can set your watch by him. I am not used to this.

Last night before he went home he said he was so happy with everything in his life that he was frightened. Fear is the unwanted companion at the picnic. I have longed for the kind of intimacy I have with Ragan all my life, and the sweetness of having it in late middle age—or early old age—is so much greater for having done without it until now.

❧

Last night, Ragan and I decided on the spur of the moment to drive to the ocean. It was a lovely time, filled with easy silences and unself-conscious revelations. "Here is what you must do to make this relationship work," I said. Before I could supply him with the requirement, he said, "Love and adore you forever?" "Yes," I replied. "And you," he countered, "must accept me for who I am." "I do," I said.

❧

Yesterday morning I picked a bunch of Queen Anne's lace from the roadside. What a miracle of design it is: delicate explosions of flowerets, some at full bloom, others still curled tightly inside spiky green strands that fall backward, like the popped ribs of an umbrella in a windstorm, when the flower is unfurled.

❧

For you, as for everyone, there is only one road that can lead to God and this is the fidelity to remain constantly true to yourself, to what you feel is highest in you. Do not worry about the rest. The road will open before you as you go. —*Pierre Teilhard de Chardin,*
Letters to Two Friends, 1926–1952

This morning I am picking words like fruit from other people's trees. I am grateful that there exists the capacity to dine off ideas. This great word swap keeps me from being impoverished by too few thoughts of my own to sustain me.

Reading from Norman Vincent Peale's *The Power of Positive Thinking* (to show a writing student where he is pulling his punches), I was struck by a thought I need—that big prayers are required for big results. I have neglected to act upon this fact. To humbly, confidently lay out all my requests, to pray about and for them, has a power that I have been neglecting to use.

Ragan back from a Florida business trip. This morning he sleeps happily upstairs while Bear and I are downstairs in the living room. Such domesticity! A quiet evening reading Orwell's essays (me) and the newspaper (Ragan), then to bed and going to sleep in loving arms. I wonder how many embraces it will take to equal the number of embraces denied. Already I am healed, unaware until now that I was wounded.

Last night, after putting supper on the table, I was smitten by the beauty of the scene: the white plates and napkins on a checkered red cotton tablecloth, the flowers in their small glass bottles, the smell of onions and rosemary-rubbed chicken, steam rising from the corn in the late-afternoon light.

Ragan on the subject of humility: "It reminds you that you don't have all the answers and that it is all right not to— nobody does. Actually, it's a relief."

I hadn't thought of humility this way. I've always lived as if finding (and holding on to) the answers was the point of life. But it suddenly struck me that true enlightenment consists in being empty, not full, of answers, that people who are full of answers must drag them around all day like an overpacked suitcase, with no room for anything new.

A decision yesterday—to give up hard liquor. I have been waiting for that late-afternoon gin and tonic with too much eagerness. The impetus was my concern that the effects of alcohol upon my brain were too deleterious to risk it any longer. I poured an almost full bottle of Tanqueray down the kitchen sink.

In California with Ragan

No journal entries for over a week. Love has swept me off the page. The reflective life is apparently no match for the life I am leading now. Yesterday, sitting on the deck outside of Sam's Anchor Café in Tiburon, watching seagulls wheel above the tables in search of food, I couldn't believe our good fortune—all of San Francisco, gleaming like a sugar palace on the bay, the sailboats keeling over with wind, the sunny water and skies; there is no more beautiful sight. Molly Keil's house, with every window full of boats, the elegance of the old Keil house flanked by tulip poplars, eucalyptus, and palms, was both dreamlike and real.

IN CARMEL

Alone in Francesca's kitchen, a mat of fog over the town. Yesterday, Francesca, Shary Farr, and I took a picnic to Garland Park in Carmel Valley. We reclined by the river and had lunch (how many friendships are cemented by the same taste in food?) and I read aloud Pablo Neruda's "Ode to My Socks" from *Ten Poems to Set You Free*. They were as quiet as children during story time, with the water softly purling over the river stones nearby. Then I took a walk and sat down on a bench and watched the birch trees.

The leaves caught the sun and tossed it with the wind, a million cradles rocking a million slips of sun back and forth, trees on fire with silver-green light. The dusty summer air smelled of all the boring years when I dreamed of action. It is an earthy, sweet smell, that travels directly to that part of my brain where whole years of my childhood wait to be remembered: summer nights, oak trees, wool blankets, screen porches, burnt toast, the scent of my own arm as I rested my chin upon it and stared into the distance.

For what seems like the first time in my life, I have begun to see, really see, birds. It was a blazingly blue-and-white day, with sandpipers making quilted tracks across the wet sand. A pair of egrets flew so low that a wave caught their wings before they sheared off in perfect formation. At Stewart's Beach I watched the pelicans wheel around the sky, sometimes folding their wings to lower their altitude, then resting on the currents to glide gracefully to the earth. Seagulls have a different method of flying. They land like parasailors in one swift downward motion until their feet touch the sand. The sky is a parallel universe, full of activity I had been too earthbound to notice. Before now, I was like the man on the beach slowly sweeping his metal detector over the sand, my eye and mind taken up with lower things. Near him, a group of four people sit in beach chairs facing the sea, each one of them buried in a book. This seems a bit like coming to a symphony only to wind up talking on the phone.

Francesca and I stayed up late into the night, clearing the air of her grievances about me. They were all about neatness: stains on sweaters, coffee grounds on the floor and in the kitchen drawers, being too proprietary about a house that isn't mine. I spoke to Ragan about my sloppiness this morning on the phone and he said he knew this about me but considered it part of the package. But what is frustrating to me is to realize that my notion of real, steady improvement in this department is so far from the requirements of most people. Truly, I don't care about getting a hole in my tights as long as the ratio between holes and tights isn't too equal. Holes happen. In the end, Francesca and I repledged ourselves to each other. Our mutual affection is not in doubt, which makes these talks easier.

Dinner with my friend Julie Beck, who seems much less encumbered. Her house in Corral de Tierra sits on a hill overlooking the bare California hills. Below, the oaks twist in the light, each tree a separate expression against wheat-colored summer grass. She has created a perfect pause of a house, each room pressed into silence by the view. It is cool and dry and brilliant, rather like Julie herself.

∾

BACK HOME AGAIN

Yesterday, I read to the Immaculates from Jacques Lusseyran's essays on blindness. What a touching group they are. The highlight was Nancy's statement that she was actually grateful for her blindness. "I wouldn't exchange the gifts I've received for seeing," she declared. All over town, these quiet, sanctifying processes are going on, right beneath my eyes.

∾

A conversation with Justin, who said he loved Ragan. "Is that because you don't have to worry about me?" I asked. "Not at all," he said. "I love him because he brings you joy."

Sunday night, after dinner with Ragan's grandchildren, Bennett and Lucas backed me into the kitchen and Lucas asked, "Do you like Pops?" "Yes," I said. "Do you like him enough to marry him?" asked Bennett. (They were grinning from ear to ear.) "What?" I exclaimed, feigning shock and surprise. This made them laugh delightedly. "Pops said you would blush," said Lucas. "Did he put you up to this?" I asked. They didn't answer but Lucas pointed a finger at me and said with mock sternness, "Saint James the Less Church, eight o'clock tomorrow. Be there!"

It was another warm family night with the three grandsons in front of the fire. Bennett, plump and cuddly, fit easily by my side on the sofa. Lucas, always thoughtful, looked into the fire and said, "I'm having a good time." Matthew, the bookworm, was curled up in a chair with *Harry Potter*. When a house is used to capacity it is like a heart being exercised well. Sitting next to Ragan, who took over Matthew's place in a game of Chinese checkers, I touched the back of his hand. He looks so happy and handsome in the bosom of his family.

I had a long conversation yesterday afternoon with Cousin Irene. There are some places in the heart that only a member of one's family can fill. Irene has a good mind and sense of humor, which seems to be improving with age. She has just turned seventy! My glamorous San Francisco cousin!

All unhappiness stems from a lack of freedom. It can be a mental lack or a physical lack. I am not, for instance, free to plan too far ahead in my life because I don't yet know whether it will include a husband. Neither do I feel free to treat Ragan's family as mine, because it isn't. Sharing the same roof when children are here is not possible, which saddens me. So all the above comes under the category of what I don't have. But what I also do not have is coherence. I am so unfree at this time in my mind that I feel dangerous, as if I will say something that will sabotage my own and Ragan's happiness needlessly.

Last night, on the second anniversary of Mom's death, Ragan asked me to marry him, something he didn't know he was going to do when he sat down with me before the fire. Punching through his fear, he proposed, and all because I wouldn't let him buy me clothes at Nordstrom's for Christmas because I wasn't his wife.

THANKSGIVING DAY

Last night I found red roses between the front and storm doors. *May 20th will be our day* said the card.

I am aware of needing to make myself psychologically ready for marriage. There needs to be room for it. At the moment, the comfort of being together is intense. The unfamiliar, unexpected security of having a partner washes over me, changes the landscape the way flowers do. But when I do not spend enough time alone, I begin to wither. Solitude keeps me porous and pliable, the way seawater keeps kelp from drying out.

It has been two weeks since we decided to marry. This last week was a surprisingly flat, even negative experience. Having burst out of a room that was too small, now we are in a room too vast. Can we fill it?

Elizabeth Ely's comment about Ragan: "He could lead a small life but he's not made for it."

I have prayed for the opportunity to love a man deeply and it has been granted, but to do it I must dig much deeper into my reserves of love than I've ever had to dig before. Last night I looked at him from this place of commitment for the first time. I see!

READING FROM PEMA CHODRON'S *WHEN THINGS FALL APART*

The truth you believe in and cling to makes you unavailable to hear anything new. Make friends with that clinging. Get to know it and it will let go by itself.

My thought: When you climb up a mountain, each cleft in the face gives you a toehold that enables you to lift yourself higher. But the minute you are higher, the cleft below becomes useless or irrelevant except as a marker. The next, higher place to put your foot is what you must search for now. So it is with any truth. If we cling to it, instead of using it to gain greater enlightenment, we remain in the same place.

I wonder if the process of aging doesn't bring as its chief gift the capacity to separate our intellect from our feelings. A sixteen-year-old can know one thing but be emotionally incapable of acting upon it. At sixteen, the emotional needs must come first if the heart is to survive. Perhaps this is true at every age, but at sixty-six, I am no longer hungry in that old starving way. Even if all my sources of comfort were to vanish, I would know how to create new ones.

2005

NEW YEAR'S DAY, IN CARMEL WITH RAGAN

Yesterday morning things came to a head; in Safeway, I felt briefly as if I were going to faint. The cause? A sudden sense that I had made a terrible mistake: I was with the wrong man in the wrong life. Ragan's temper was flaring at every small thing—tailgating drivers, the construction going on next door. Finally, back home, I expressed my own anger, telling him that I would not live with this *ever*. We discussed the fact that he views a wife as the lover—confidante of his whole life. I said that put too much pressure on me. I asked him what he thought was the purpose of his life. He didn't know. After retreating to his room, he finally came out and said that there were three ways for him to deal with this—run, ignore it, or face it. He chose the last.

I must remember that what Ragan thinks and what he reveals are two different things most of the time. It would be a mistake to underestimate him.

I am finding R sweet again. He is trying manfully to get above his moods, his temper, his easily bruised feelings. I am not sure what I am trying to overcome, but here I am sleeping beside him every night, living alongside him every day, and like a pair of threads we are weaving ourselves into each other's lives.

This morning the wind is whistling through the trees and around the cottage. The kettle mimics the sound with a whistle of its own. A fire burns quietly in the grate, filling the room with the smell of wood smoke.

I think the temptation or desire to control Ragan's perceptions of life, to make him see it my way, is the major way I sin against humility.

I am learning how to live with someone. I have lived life for so long on my own terms, without anyone in the other room, coughing, running water, letting me know he is there. And this morning, as I sit here in the living room, journal on my knee, I am grateful for the lessons. All the ways in which we are different remain. Perhaps we will decide that they are too many to surmount, that we are asking too much of ourselves to marry. But I am also aware of something else that seems to be pushing to the front of my consciousness. Could it be the simple sincerity of his love for me? Are my fears of being cut off from life, tethered and curtailed, lodged more in my imagination than in reality? How often we equate one with the other. I am content to wait, to let time tell me what I don't know.

I'm beginning to realize anew that every day must be created from nothing. This is particularly true when living with someone else. Peace must continually be drawn out of discord. Something as small as making a cup of coffee can get in the way. ("Let me make it." "No, you don't make it strong enough." "Yes, I do.")

To quote Mary Oliver, our time here in Carmel has "thickened with incident." In the process, Ragan and I are becoming companions. A sign of the increasing ease and intimacy we have with each other is found in my ability to sit in the same room with him, as I am now, in silence, which must be a relief to him. He has never had so many demands upon him to think and communicate. But being able to have real conversations means too much to me to go without it.

❧

We took Ragan's granddaughter Brittany and my niece Devon down the coast for dinner. Big Sur in the winter has bright green pastures, full rivers, dark damp woods. We rush down the highway in a heated car, the way one rushes past a truth that is powerful and silent and not altogether friendly. Reality is on the other side of the window.

Teenage girls are inscrutable. At dinner, Ragan and I labored to get Devon and Brittany to talk, to uncork them. But they sat across the table, mostly silent and unconscious of our desperate conversational ploys. A lot of panning for a little gold.

❧

Just before sundown Ragan and I drove down to Garrapata Ridge in Big Sur and took a road high up the side of the mountain to a friend's house. Such sheer cliffs and sheer beauty is rarely found in combination. There was one harrowing switchback curve after another, each slice in the mountain revealing another view of deep canyons, pleated hills, and sudden thousand-foot drops. The house was a welcome lantern at the top. The second time I drive up that ridge, I won't be so terrified. We ended farther down Route 1, at Deetjen's, my favorite restaurant in the world, for dinner. In this rustic low-ceilinged roadside cottage by the ocean, with a roaring fire and a flute quintet playing quietly through the speakers, everything was harmonious and real.

Ash Wednesday. Awoke early, worrying over my inability to make time for what is important. Everything hangs on good health, and it has been months since I've exercised. How to lead a contemplative life while married, how to lead a physically disciplined life, how to lead the life of a working writer. These are the questions I would like to address. The underlying fear of exertion has always slowed me down. Why the fear of inactivity doesn't hold the same charge I do not know.

Last night I was kept awake by the prospect of chaos and change—the great disarray into which Ragan and I are heading as we try to combine two households. Just the small amount of chaos redoing the upstairs bathroom entails is difficult. How will it be when entire walls are sledge-hammered to the ground? I don't know, but this morning, with a cup of coffee in my hand and a silent house, it seems doable.

Last night, Ragan and I celebrated my birthday early at the Manakin Grill, where we had gotten back together in May of last year. It is a quieter one than last year, but what deep joy I feel with Ragan, who has given me so many reasons to love him. No one could have prepared me for this.

"Last year," said Ellen, "he was the guy who brought the cake. This year he *is* the cake."

ᕮᕮ

Four days in New York with Ragan. Each day was a renewal of an old friendship: Nancy, Mary, Molly, Gene. But coming back to Ashland was a relief, like walking into a spacious room after living in a broom closet. New York felt like home—Zabar's, the Apthorp, gazing out of Nancy's window onto the street full of nineteenth-century brownstones, the subways—but my sensibilities have shifted. Looking at Ragan in his Stetson, towering above the New Yorkers in a subway car rattling toward Union Square, made me smile.

Wedding plans unfold with news of who is coming. Why my journal seems to be so empty of meaning concerns me. This morning I picked up a news story about Mary-Kate and Ashley Olsen's wardrobe and read it *with interest*. God, how the mind loves to constrict. The effort it takes to stretch either the mind or the body is so easy to avoid.

ᕮᕮ

Last night as I lay in bed, I began to pray for myself as if it were an entirely new idea, never before thought of, as in *Oh, here's a possibility. Why not try this, not only for myself but my children, and anyone I love or care about, even the world?* Why do I have such a feeling about prayer's efficacy now? Is it because the weak efforts I've allowed myself to make have borne fruit? Is there a connection? What I felt as I lay there silently, wordlessly, asking for virtues I do not have, was hope.

❧

This is an entirely new life I am leading, the life of a couple. My edges are being rounded, my sensibilities dulled or deepened. I can't tell which.

Ragan just came into the living room to read me Mary Oliver's poem, "When Death Comes." (*When it's over, I want to say all my life I was a bride married to amazement.*) He had to read it slowly so his voice didn't wobble with emotion. He is becoming "the bride married to amazement" in that poem.

❧

The wedding invitations have arrived, in letter-perfect condition. I told the woman at Meade's Office Supply where I ordered them that coming to pick them up was like calling the gynecologist to find out if I was pregnant. Ragan, during my two-day absence in Washington, had a bout of doubt, brooding over whether he would be able to fulfill his duties as a husband. He had righted his boat by the time we talked on the phone last night.

Two months from now we will be married. I see no turning back, although I do have concerns that will probably always be there about the rightness of it. Ragan is clear that it is my decision. "You know what you're getting," he said yesterday, meaning that he is a country-bred, unclassically educated, small-town man.

I asked him to tell his life story from the standpoint of his evolving consciousness. "Well, I guess you could say I had my head in the sand until I was sixty. Then I began to wake up." This is what I see as so positive, that he is a man committed to change. But am I somehow making more of this than it warrants?

My mind and emotions are being pulled like taffy between different considerations that revolve around house and finances. But when I put my mind in a higher place and think about what I hope to be to Ragan as his wife, the aperture widens.

The first real morning of spring. The air is cool; the light fills up the grass, which is soft and bright green. Yesterday afternoon, I put the wedding invitations in the mail. Now they're flying across the country, around the neighborhood, creating a web of connections between my life and Ragan's. Great happiness is being created by this union, apart from our own. It gives both my sons a feeling of stability. Eliza is glad her mother is being taken care of. My friends are semi-incredulous that I have found such a loving man at such a late date.

This feeling of doubt, that I am doing something I will regret, washes over me, makes me scared. How can I know which of my many feelings I should follow? Could I be choosing security over truth at this late stage? I am, in many ways, too much influenced by others' opinions. "He's a catch," said Dolo. "Do you know how hard it is to find a presentable man like that?" exclaimed Edie. "What's not to love?" asked Debbie. But more importantly, it is I who gradually felt his absence when we were separated and felt joy when he returned. Yet, and yet . . . just now I am less sure than I want to be.

One other connection that discomfits me—the relationship between love and loss. When I sense ambivalence in Ragan, my own doubts are replaced with the fear of losing him. So I am mystified. Could the conventions of society, wanting to be like the others, be at the bottom of my decision? Can I be someone's partner and still be free? I don't think there are any easy answers, but I do know that the commitment to love someone must go deeper than the easy decision to care for someone when the emotional tide is high.

Once again the ocean is calm and I can see serenely to the bottom. The feeling of good fortune, of being gently held, not clutched, returns. Justin, ever vigilant, phones me daily to take my emotional temperature, calling my fears the result of a horrendous first marriage. He so wants me to be with Ragan, a feeling universally shared. I will be glad when we are on the other side.

Some thoughts too intimate to be put on paper, the sense of being cherished as I sleep against his side at night. This is a man who is never too tired to kiss me tenderly on my head as he is going off to sleep. Thirty-five years ago, I longed for that kind of easy exchange between a husband and wife. Now, in far different circumstances, it has come to me.

❧

Yesterday all my fears and apprehensions came to a head when I was sitting in my kitchen with my friend Carol. Just as she was about to leave, I grabbed her hands and asked if she would pray for me. She sat back down and prayed out loud while I listened, tears leaking from my eyes. Then we sat together and talked.

Carol told me how terrified she had been six weeks before her marriage. "I didn't want to go through with it," she said. Up in her parents' attic, she burst into tears and dropped to her knees and prayed for guidance. At one point, she heard a voice inside her say quietly, "Love him. Trust in me." She felt momentarily at peace. But then her worries came back, along with fresh tears. Once more, the inner voice repeated, "Love him. Trust in me." Again, peace was replaced by fear. Finally, the third time this happened she stopped crying, said "all right," and let her fears go.

Until now I have never thought about what it really means to let go of one's fears, as if they were reins on a horse that was running away with me. My fears have not gone away but I am trying to deal with them honestly.

❧

AT THE BISHOP'S RANCH IN HEALDSBURG, CALIFORNIA, FOR MY WRITING SEMINAR

The beauty of this place fills me: a bright swath of fog lying upon the fields in the early morning, the sun brushing the wisteria-hung arbor, turning the purple flowers gold, the gentle layering of hills and mountain range. As the heat increases, so does the smell of lavender. I think of my mother, how she loved what I am looking at and how much I miss having her with me.

The earnest desire and serious work of the writers here bring tears to my eyes at times. There is such beauty in their stories; as they read them aloud I can see an invisible cord wrapping itself around each listener, making one heart out of many, beating in the same sympathetic rhythm as each story draws to an end.

My premarriage mood of doom has lifted. Perhaps, as one student observed, this is because Mercury had been retrograde and only went out of it two days ago. Whatever the reason, my belief in my marriage to Ragan has returned. It did not happen without his help. A deeper than usual letter from him, enclosing another Mary Oliver poem about rowing toward life, made the difference.

In North Beach at the Café Trieste

This is the San Francisco that is unglazed and unfazed by the tidal wave of wealth that has rolled over the rest of the city. Even the cappuccino is cheaper. The customers are scruffier and more thoughtful-looking than most San Franciscans you see.

Upon returning home, I told Ragan that I still had doubts about the rightness of getting married, never mind that the wedding itself was only a few weeks away. Ragan reassured me that, whatever happened, he would understand and survive. His loving kindness stunned me. On the brink of losing him, I saw the depth of loss it would entail.

The way truth emerges like an involuntary sob surprises me. The heart, knowing what the intellect cannot come to on its own, had chosen Ragan long before the rest of me assented. After an anxious twenty-four hours, during which time I worried that my endless vacillations had finally worn him out, I emerged into the sun. Save for a now-diagnosed case of shingles. I am determined to keep my joy separate from my distress. My doubts about marriage have been replaced with gratitude. The thought of losing Ragan so horrified me that I came, albeit at the last minute, to my senses. Fortunately, R had the room in him to let me go through the process. As the days count down to the wedding, I am at last having a bridal time of it, feeling anticipatory. My life once more looks like my own, only larger.

Such happiness! I am blessed to have Ragan as the man I love, who loves me. It is early, 5 A.M., and I have come downstairs to be with the quiet. But knowing that such a deeply loving man, soon to be my husband, sleeps upstairs, fills me with gratitude and astonishment. At sixty-six to be me!

My friend Valerie called, saying that she and Michael want to give me his mother's piano, that gleaming black beauty I surreptitiously played when I visited them last year, as a wedding present. I cannot remember a better gift in my entire life. I told her that this means we will be friends for life. "We have to be. It's like giving me your child."

The small RSVP envelopes are still coming in. The circle is defining itself. Almost everybody who is or has been important in my life will be here. An image of ships laden with gold slowly approaching the harbor is how I feel about them.

How to handle money matters continues to be unresolved on an emotional level. My fear is that I may feel like a pauper in my own house once we're married. When one spouse has considerably more money than the other, money is power. I don't see any good solution except to change one's view of money itself.

Both Ragan and I are moving beyond the need to think about bowing out. "Let's not talk this way anymore," I said yesterday. He agreed. We continue to work away at the details of the prenuptial agreement, yet I am, I told him last night, beyond that, too. I am inwardly assured that the essentials are there.

Looking for something Mom might have written to put into the wedding program, I came across so many letters of mine, including eulogies I'd written, that reminded me of how short life is: a note to Paul Sigmund after his mother died, tributes for Ann Buchwald and Rita Wall. Rehearsing for the wedding at Saint James the Less, I thought of the church filling for Nina's and Jay's funerals. Lying in Ragan's arms, I know this comfort will end, too.

It occurs to me that there are false emotional safety nets that should not be used. R's desire to make our marriage work and his fear of failure is one of them. My knowledge of this fear could cause me to rely on it as a form of protection that has nothing to do with our love for each other.

Eight days to the wedding! I have gone from terror to delight. All my children are coming. I am going to be seeing all three of them under one tent along with so many cherished friends from my whole life that it may be a bit overwhelming.

Last night Ragan said he thought we should stay apart from now until our wedding. I agreed. It seems appropriate and, given the family members pouring in soon, practical. Ragan put his arms around me at the door and said, "I love you so much and I want to take care of you"—this after admitting that it would be simpler to be single with his dog and books.

Ragan is as peaceful as I am about the wedding. I am aware that he is not a young man. The way he walks is slower than a man twenty years younger. But I am so in love with his mien and manner. There is something particularly endearing about the way he strides purposefully across a street, his elbows rowing the air, eyes gazing at the road ahead. After being alone for most of my life, I cannot quite believe that I'm being given a companion with whom to end my days.

Up early to work on the liturgy for the wedding ceremony. Our decision to live in our separate houses is a wise one. Yet the longing to be in one place together increases. Last night he came in and said, "Only ninety-three hours left." Spoken like an engineer, but it shows his eagerness. How miraculous that my own certainty has held firm.

One way or another, the house and garden are getting ready for the wedding. Porch doors have been painted, flowers planted. The lawn was just cut and is a velvety green, the envy of the neighborhood. Who is this person I'm becoming?

The wedding festivities roll toward us, but we are unperturbed. Sitting here, with the dearness of this house still unchanged, I am aware of the imminent transformation—of myself, of the garden (soon to be covered with white tents) and in a few weeks the house itself, when remodeling begins. At yoga class last night I looked at my feet. They seemed older. This morning, looking at my hands resting in my lap, I saw how elderly they were, too. And yet we are about to be newlyweds. Our age only intensifies the joy.

We are married! The prewedding party on Thursday night brought so many loved people together. Friday was the wedding—for family and a few close friends—followed by dinner in the garden at Ragan's house. Rain forced us inside, but being under one roof only intensified the experience. Saturday was a blow-out neighborhood wedding party under a big white tent with a dance floor on the lawn behind my house. It was everything I had hoped it would be—a warm, full house with such happiness in the eyes of everyone there. The three toasts I'll remember: my cousin Johnny's words about our relationship being one of two souls, Jill's acerbic toast about this being a warm-up for the eulogy I'd asked her to deliver, and Chris Clark's a capella singing of "Drink to Me Only with Thine Eyes." It was an artless act of generosity and he caught the whole room in his hands.

Ragan's daughter Meg read from a hanging quilt she had embroidered with advice from our grandchildren about how to have a happy marriage. ("Hug and cuddle a lot," said five-year-old Rhys. "Don't fight, and love each other—just a friendly suggestion," said seven-year-old Bennett. "Never let your spouse start the day without a cup of coffee," said eleven-year-old Matthew.) But mostly it was Ragan, whose love was a bright beacon throughout it all.

Now, on a Monday morning, the house is quiet, rooms of flowers everywhere, and a husband is in the kitchen reading the paper. We exchanged letters just before we walked down the aisle. His was so radiant with feeling and joy. "I have never loved so deeply or wisely before," it began. His ring to me is inscribed *Te semper amo et adoro. Ragan.* Mine, *To Ragan, with all my heart, Phyllis.* His is more unique.

We are in Bermuda, in a pink two-room villa overlooking a harbor, most of which belongs to Cambridge Beaches, where we are staying. The air is soft, the sun bright, and the Bermudians almost without exception a happy, friendly people. On the bus into Hamilton yesterday, the driver danced in his seat to some salsa on the radio. He honked at every other bus driver and embraced old women coming up the steps. The passengers were equally friendly. Bermuda itself seems far less British. One still sees men in knee socks and shorts, but huge sky-blocking cruise ships rest in Hamilton Harbor.

Trimingham's sells the same cashmere sweaters you can get in Macy's. This alters the character of the town.

Being a married woman seems so easy because of Ragan. Everywhere I look there are other ring-wearing couples eating breakfast, reading the newspaper, playing croquet. Am I feeling relief at being like everyone else? Certainly I feel more protected. But I don't feel less free. That is the difference between marrying early and remarrying late. In between one and the other I found my life.

On the "morning beach" with bright sun, calm water, and soft sand. The couples aspect of this place is beginning to seem overdone. So many gold bands, like ducks who have been tagged for identification. Yet I do feel supported in a way I never thought would happen by a man who really does seem to have my interests at heart. It is so different to live with a man, to see his shaving gear, his shirts, his pipe next to my things. I think, because of the long years alone, it will always feel a little thrilling, like becoming famous or rich late in life.

R's sixty-ninth birthday. We both agreed that sixty-nine sounds older than seventy. Went to the Cambridge Beach library this rainy morning, gathered up a half dozen books, everything from Balzac to Stephen Spender, with some Thornton Wilder and Ian Trevor as well. The Spender journals immerse me in another life I cannot lead except vicariously. The black-and-white photos of Sartre, Eliot, Auden, and Isherwood are from a family album not my own. But I can snoop and identify parts of their lives and ideas as being like my own.

During this week, Ragan has experienced a bit of insecurity with me, the result of my being quieter than usual,
which he interprets as being a withdrawal *from* him. "No," I
countered, "it is a withdrawal *into* myself." I do not think the
same need exists in him. Quiet can be the two of us reading silently. But he prefers that I be nearby. I need regular
time without anybody else around in order to feel restored.
Now, as I sit in our pretty living room with the rain gone and
the room to myself, I feel such peace, which is all the greater
because of Ragan being my husband and being away at the
gym, simultaneously.

One of the benefits of getting married so late is that
certain life lessons are already very firmly established. One of
them, that you are responsible for your own happiness, comes
to mind now. In an earlier time I would have taken responsibility for my husband's happiness, too. But the wiser, truer
course is to create one's own and then share it. Otherwise, one
winds up trying to track down every shadow that passes across
your husband's face, as if it belonged to you instead of him.

We took a ferry to Hamilton, which is a dingy town with
cheap souvenirs and bad coffee. We had no reason to go, other
than to give ourselves a ferry ride and do something besides
take naps and wait for the next meal. But coming back on the
island bus from the dockyards to Mangrove Bay, we sat across
from a young teenage boy, fair-skinned, dark-eyed, and wiry,
who reminded me of something important.

His face was alive with curiosity. Everyone who got
on the bus was gone over with wide-open eyes. He was taking

the world in as fast as it was presented to him. What a sharp contrast he was to the other passengers, most of them elderly, whose faces and eyes were closed down except for a narrow opening to let in enough light to see by. My mother maintained the alertness of that young boy to the end of her life. It is not age but awareness that makes the difference—and a lack of judgmentalness. I wonder, if I could see my own face, how open and nonjudgmental it would be.

We are home from the honeymoon. Being cast upon one's own as we were for seven days rinsed my mind of some of the impurities of modern life that I had gotten too dependent upon—gossip magazines, nonstop NPR, the phone. For stimulation, there were books, conversation, and thinking. I found myself interested, as I had been as a child, in what I saw on the road—tangles of nasturtiums, squashed cherries, bay-grape leaves stiff as leather paddles on the grass. Sitting on the terrace overlooking the bay I meditated on the fact of our mutability, how almost every person in the restaurant will be wiped off the stage in fifty years or less. Yet we sit and butter our toast as if we are immortal.

This is the beginning of my new life.

This morning, as I poured hot water onto fresh coffee grounds, I thought of all the married couples who have come together for the same reasons: comfort, company, safety. How much are we motivated by the powerful desire to feel safe? And is feeling safe and unafraid the same thing?

❧

A beautiful congratulatory note from my friend Kitty, enclosing a silver-framed shamrock and a quotation from G. K. Chesterton:

The power of hoping through everything, the knowledge that the soul survives its adventures, that great inspiration comes to the middle-aged, God has kept that good wine until now. It is from the backs of the elderly gentlemen that the wings of the butterfly should burst.

She ended the note with, "So soar!"

Along with this came a note in the shape of a butterfly from Nancy Newhouse, saying how much she loved the wedding party. The backwash of that long moment continues to bring good things in on the tide.

❧

Distressing news from Italy. My Siena friend Jennifer Storey has breast cancer that has spread to her lymph nodes. She is caught up in many different emotions, including intense fear. I cannot take pleasure in my own life, knowing what is happening to her.

I am holding the volume of Emerson's essays that Jennifer took from me in Italy last year and made whole again, regluing the pages and strengthening the spine with a new red leather binding. Now it will last a long time. This is what friends do for each other. We strengthen each other's spines.

❧

The process of transferring and merging two separate lives into one, physically and emotionally, is a daily challenge. I wonder if I am not losing a certain jauntiness (my daughter Eliza's favorite word to describe herself) that being independent creates. Now that my dependence, physically, upon him has grown, it seems to me that I am too watchful of Ragan's moods, monitoring him.

Between then and now there has been another climate change—a contentment that is like an incoming tide, sliding up the sand, filling in the holes, leveling the surface. As best as I can surmise, it is a human exchange that did it, conversation on a higher level that calms my soul. Recently, Ragan said that he knows he can tell me anything that is in his heart. It takes so little now to reassure me that I am in the right place and relationship.

A metaphor catches my imagination, the idea that our bodies have "general contractors" who repair what is broken but usually on a longer lead time than we want. My ear, for instance, had fluid in it for the better part of a month. Finally, I made an appointment with the doctor, just before it cleared up on its own. My rib cage, bruised when I fell out of bed, healed on its own slow schedule, too. To extend the metaphor a bit more, if we take good care of our property, the general contractor can move more quickly, perform more efficiently.

Hurricane Katrina has wiped out the Gulf Coast areas of Alabama, Mississippi, and Louisiana. New Orleans is a city of the past. Whatever happens, it will be almost entirely new. The poor are the hardest hit, trapped in flooded houses, drowning in attics, bodies floating in the water. The reality of losing everything you have and not being able to return to where you lived—having the slate entirely erased—is not something I'm capable of really comprehending. In my world, there are so many avenues of escape.

I am beginning to really see why the first part of my life was so slow and creative. There was little except books and the radio, with an occasional Saturday afternoon movie into which I could escape. This left me uncomfortably in my own skin, with my imagination as the only escape route. Restlessness and the aching desire to experience new things were part of my daily life. The outer quiet was broken only by the sounds of footsteps, scraping chairs, the swish of water, and other mostly human-generated noises that were not distracting. The phone rarely, if ever, rang for me.

This morning, I watched a yellow leaf drift to the ground like a butterfly, twisting in the air as if it had wings, and I thought of Mother, who loved autumn with the air full of leaves whenever the wind blew. It excited her, the way the prospect of going someplace new—or dying—excited her. "The body has its fears," she admitted. But she herself had none.

This morning Ragan read from Roger Housden's essay on marriage. Love, Housden writes, is not pleasure but work, and since it is work that makes us happy, love is necessarily the hardest work of all.

Last night we had our first dinner on Duncan Street [my house, which was extensively remodeled after we got married]. Later, Ragan gazed into the living room, newly slipcovered and blooming with lighted lamps, and declared it welcoming. So the transition has begun.

Notes from our trip to Molly and Mark's house in Bedford Hills, New York

Molly's largeness of spirit, coupled with an honest mind and compassionate eye for the foibles of those she loves, make her so lovable to me. I consider her an ace up my sleeve, someone who makes it easier for me to live my life knowing she is there.

Their recently adopted four-year-old son, Nando, is a small, observant elf, black-eyed and endearing. Their seven-year-old adopted daughter, P-Quy, confided to her mother that everyone loves him "because he's so cute—and he is, Mom." Being in Molly and Mark's house is like floating down the river in an inner tube. Hot water, thick towels, down pillows, and fat shrimp with cocktail sauce. Conversation flies around like a birdie in a badminton game. I'm beginning to realize that perhaps I am as important to Molly as she is to me.

∾

Here in Ashland, the sounds of hammers and trains. Fall leaves sift through the air. I am content to make this home. Ragan is a good husband. We fit amazingly well, almost because of the differences.

This morning, searching for an inspired bit of material to launch these pages, I opened Henry Miller's *On Writing*. There it was:

The creative individual (in wrestling with his medium) is supposed to experience a joy which balances, if it does not outweigh, the pain and anguish which accompany the struggle to express himself. He lives his work, we say. But this unique kind of life varies extremely with the individual. It is only in the measure that he is aware of more life, the life abundant, that he may be said to live in his work. If there is no realization, there is no purpose or advantage in substituting the imaginative life for the purely adventurous one of reality. Everyone who lifts himself above the activities of the daily round does so not only in the hope of enlarging his field of experience, or even of enriching it, but of quickening it.

That, in Miller's beautifully strung-together words, is what we're after—the joy of quickening the dead, of bringing something inert to life. Once you have experienced it, you want it again.

∾

Packed and ready for Italy. A part of me is already there, with my broken Italian, making my way around Rosia, admiring the cyclamen along the banks that flank the winding road to Orgia.

It always amazes me how one decision can trigger so many others. My going to Italy caused Ragan's daughter, Meg, to decide to come, too. She will meet her best friend in Paris. We are always paving the way for each other, although it takes a long time in one's development to grasp the truth that being responsible for your own life is so much more exhilarating than waiting for someone else to pave the way, make it right.

❧

The flight across the Atlantic was fairly bumpy. The plane creaked like an old ship. Outside, the sky was jammed with stars, clear and fixed against the wild fishtailing of our airplane.

A missed plane connection due to slow customs. I am stuck at Gatwick for the night. Sleepless at 2 A.M. I finished Kurt Vonnegut's book, *A Man Without a Country*. I don't think there is one word of it that I disagree with, and much of it is so sublime I want to snatch it up and engrave it on everyone's mind.

Vonnegut's thoughts on the power of the imagination (he can look at a face and see stories; others only see a face) makes me realize—again!—how easily it can fall into disuse. The streets are full of people who don't use their imaginations for anything more than to imagine dinner, or how a new sweater could change their mood. I speak firsthand.

❧

I wonder if the process of aging doesn't bring as its chief gift the capacity to separate our intellect from our feelings. A sixteen-year-old can know one thing but be emotionally incapable of acting upon it. At sixteen, the emotional needs must come first if the heart is to survive. Perhaps this is true at every age, but at sixty-six, I am no longer hungry in that old starving way. Even if all my sources of comfort were to vanish, I would know how to create new ones. A sixteen-year-old doesn't know this about herself. A thirty-two-year-old has trouble knowing it, too. Instinctively, we hang on to what we've got for fear that there won't be any more. Who or what teaches us this? To be alive and standing should be enough to prove that life will support us when we move toward it. But there is always the fear that the safety net will have a hole in it, that we will slip through and be lost.

∽

AT SPANNOCCHIA

Another wonderful group, six women and one man. This morning, Julie's notes about her family's dinners were the most powerful. While everyone else is out walking, she has gone back to her room to write, as have I. But about what? The silence, broken only by a pair of flies and my pen on paper, has not spoken to me yet. But I am comfortable with emptiness. There is something very healing about this small austere room, this wooden desk and chair, white walls, and terra-cotta floor. It is all I need or want at this moment, except for a quickening of the creative impulse.

Today I spent several hours, with one nap in the middle, writing. All I can say about it is that I kneaded the material, remembered the rules, eliminated, put back in, rewrote, and rewrote again. The spark did not appear, but just knowing that I was at work provided its own flame of a sort.

Later, I took a walk down the road, where at several spots I searched for chestnuts. On the way down the hill, I found a pocketful. Coming home, looking in the same spots, I found more. The eye is not as careful as we think. It takes many passes over the same material to see it all. True for both chestnuts and writing.

A seamless week: beautiful weather, flowing creativity, and an easy blending of personalities. Each person, including our one nonwriter, Tim, has had something very important to add to the group, which genuinely admires one another. I am perhaps most gratified by Julie's presence. She has really surprised herself and me by her writing, her conversational abilities, and the way she seems to love being here.

This is our last writing day. Everyone has found at least one assignment in which they have been able to "reach water." Writers come to Spannocchia to remember something deep inside themselves, to try—with help from the teacher and the group—to find that piece of gold or beauty that flicks by them like a darting fish.

Home. How comforting it is to be back in one's own picture. No longer do you have to search for the right preposition or coin. Travel is grueling because you have to keep moving. But it's a necessary act, like changing, because otherwise you lose the capacity to adjust to new challenges. Now, at five-thirty in the morning, with Ragan and Bear still sleeping, I am back in my wing chair, listening to the language of my old house as its pipes ping and creak in the winter cold.

❧

Signs of aging. Yesterday Dr. Everhart examined my eyes and found the very early signs of dry (the better kind to have) macular degeneration. I am aware of how much time and material is involved in maintaining myself—the medications for reflux, thyroid, cholesterol, and now macular degeneration, the exercise to keep strong, the right food to keep healthy. So much more is involved than twenty-years-ago, in what I now call my wash-and-wear days.

❧

So few new thoughts, and the ones I have fly out of my head before I can get them pinned down on paper. If I were Emerson, every specific thought would turn into a general aphorism. Instead, the aphorisms go unsaid, uncoined. With metaphors I have an easier time.

❧

Three years ago, Mom died in this house. I have just put the last remnants of her existence into a cardboard box upstairs: her special stones, a pearl shell, some other odds and ends. A husband is quietly washing dishes in the sink. I am in a new life, one in which I am so much more protected than I was before. This is a blessing I never expected to receive.

Yesterday we had our first real moving day, as boxes of books were temporarily taken out of the garage and furniture from Ragan's house was brought in. When we are done furnishing this "kingdom" I fear feeling burdened, the custodian of a life filled with scrapbooks and shoes, sofas and casserole dishes, two floors of towels, sheets, soap, hand cream, clothes, books, and curtains. In a world where there is so much poverty, we are pashas, who only have to snap our fingers for another possession to materialize.

Last night I told Ragan that he was giving me the chance to experience the difference between intense and lasting love. Given the choice, I would chose long-lasting. Perhaps in time there will be both, but a high flame takes more watching than I am prepared to do.

CHRISTMAS MORNING

R asleep on the sofa in front of the fire, Bear dozing by his side, sweet potatoes and apple pie on the stove. And where am I? My mind is off in Siena, wondering what Jennifer Storey is having for breakfast; then Carmel, where Francesca is probably just waking up. Then suddenly, I think, *Stop all this astral travel. Be present while you're peeling the yams. Notice how the flesh turns from pale yellow to mango, how the coloration of the skin has the faint look of veins.* Life is more intense when one is all here to live it.

A line from a luminous Indian movie, *Water,* in which one of the characters says of Mahatma Gandhi, "Gandhi is a man who listens to his conscience." Immediately I thought, *Do I?* What huge changes would have to come about if I did?

Later, helping my friend Elizabeth write a commence-
ment speech, I stumbled across a thought in my mind: *Use your
life to illuminate something larger.* That's it. That's what we're all
called to do.

If You Want to Keep a Journal

One of the reasons why people resist keeping a journal is because they assume it will quickly become a garbage can for all of the spoiled plans, bad news, and other dark developments in their life. The journal I keep is the spiritual equivalent of a personal light box or cheering section, which I create as I go along. This isn't to say that the pages are without pain or perplexity. The dilemmas in my life were one of the main reasons I began to keep a journal in the first place. But I use it as a tool for solving or understanding them. Whatever insights or glimpses of the truth I glean when sitting quietly in my wing chair—thinking, reading, or simply gazing out the window at a neighbor walking her dog—is what I write down.

There are other, less self-involved motives for keeping a journal. Knowing I have a place to save small pieces of beauty keeps me on the lookout for them, even in a checkout line in Safeway or on the other side of a grimy train window in the rain. These are my butterflies, halted midflight on the page. Then, there is the "journal as ragbag" use, where I store stories, anecdotes, or phrases that please my mind and ear. When my children were small, they would often say something so heartbreakingly astute or funny that I rushed to preserve it—sometimes for tomorrow's essay, which used to drive my children crazy. "Nobody else I know has this problem," wailed

Eliza, after she found herself trapped in a carful of other Brownies listening to her mother read an essay on the radio— about embarrassing her children!

Should you censor what you say? I think that goes without saying, unless your intention is to finger the person you think wants to murder you or get back at someone who has hurt your feelings, assuming they read what you write. Children of any age should be protected. Messages from the grave can too easily be misconstrued or considered the final verdict on their worth, when all you're doing is blowing off steam.

The type of journal you use is important. My advice is not to get anything too fancy. The cover might intimidate you, the paper may seem too expensive to ruin with your humble observations. For the past twenty years I have used the same five-by-seven-inch black cardboard journals with red binding that come from the Pearl River Market in Greenwich Village, New York. They are cheap and durable and fit easily into my purse when traveling. To date I have filled up at least three dozen, all neatly labeled with a pair of dates on their spines. It is the only organized thing about me.

Keeping a journal for posterity should be a minor, even inconsequential reason. The one place you want to be unselfconscious is on the pages of your private diary. That being said, there is a public dimension to writing—even if it is a laundry list—and I am not a fan of those who urge you to dump whatever comes to mind upon the page. No, no, no. Your journal should be a wise friend who helps you create your own enlightenment. Chose what you think has some merit or lasting value, so that when you reread your journal in years to come it continues to nourish you.

Some days I can think of nothing worth writing down. Fortunately, I am not alone. By my chair, I keep a small, revolving collection of essays, spiritual autobiographies, poetry, and other writers' journals to inspire me. When I'm out of fuel, they pull me out of the creek and into a broader, deeper river. My own personal list of light givers follows, which may illuminate you or not. We are different people, on the lookout for different things. But if you want your journal to have any lasting value, for yourself or others, I can only think of one rule to follow: Lean toward the light.

Reading List

Karen Armstrong. *The Spiral Staircase: My Climb Out of Darkness*. New York: Alfred A. Knopf, 2004.

W.H. Auden. *The Collected Poetry of W. H. Auden*.New York: Random House, 1945.

Marcus Aurelius. *Meditations*. New York: Viking Penguin, 1995.

Bernard Berenson. *Sunset and Twilight: From the Diaries of 1947–1958*. New York: Har-court Brace & World, 1963.

Wendell Berry. *The Selected Poems*. Washington, D.C.: Counterpoint Press, 1998.

Pema Chodron. *When Things Fall Apart: Heart Advice for Difficult Times*. Boston: Shambhala Publications, 1997.

George Crane. *Bones of the Master: A Journey to Secret Mongolia*. New York: Bantam Books, 2000.

Robert Ellsberg. *The Saints' Guide to Happiness*. New York: Farrar, Straus & Giroux, 2003.

Ralph Waldo Emerson. *Essays and Journals*. New York: Doubleday, 1968.

Hugh I'Anson Fausset. *A Modern Prelude*. London: Jonathan Cape, 1933.

F. Scott Fitzgerald. *The Great Gatsby*. New York: Charles Scribner's Sons, 1953.

John Howard Griffin. *Scattered Shadows: A Memoir of Blindness and Vision*. Maryknoll, New York: Orbis Books, 2004.

Carolyn Heilbrun. *Writing A Woman's Life*. New York: W.W. Norton & Company, 1988.

Marv and Nancy Hiles. *An Almanac for the Soul: Anthology of Hope*. Healdsburg, Calif.: Iona Center, 2008.

Etty Hillesum. *An Interrupted Life and Letters from Westerbork*. New York: Henry Holt & Co., 1996.

Roger Housden. *Ten Poems to Set You Free*. New York: Harmony Books, Random House, 2000.

Stephen King. *On Writing: A Memoir*. New York: Simon & Schuster, 2000.

Stanley Kunitz. *The Collected Poems*. New York: W.W. Norton & Co., 2000.

Giuseppe Tomasi di Lampedusa. *The Leopard*. New York: Alfred A. Knopf, 1991.

Lao-Tzu. *Tao Te Ching*. New York: Penguin Books, 1985.

Jacques Lusseyran. *And There Was Light*. New York: Parabola Books, 1998.

Rollo May. *The Courage to Create*. New York: W.W. Norton & Co., 1975.

Arthur Miller. *Timebends: A Life*. New York: Grove Press, 1987

Henry Miller. *Henry Miller on Writing*. New York: New Directions, 1964.

Czeslaw Milosz. *To Begin Where I Am,* selected essays. New York: Farrar, Straus & Giroux, 2008.

John Muir. "My First Summer in the Sierra" from *Nature Writings*. New York: The Library of America, Penguin Putnam, 1997.

Naomi Shihab Nye. *Words Under the Words: Selected Poems*. Portland, OR: Eighth Mountain Press, 1995.

Mary Oliver. *New and Selected Poems*. Boston: Beacon Press, 1992.

Blaise Pascal. *Pensées*. New York: Penguin Press, 1995.

Dorothy Berkley Phillips, Elizabeth Boyden Howes, and Lucille M. Nixon, eds. *The Choice Is Always Ours: The Classic Anthology on the Spiritual Way*. San Francisco: HarperCollins Publishers, 1989.

Jules Renard. *The Journal of Jules Renard,* edited and translated by Elizabeth Bogan and Elizabeth Roget. Portland, OR and New York: Tin House Books, 2008.

Stephen Spender. *Journals: 1939–1983*. New York: Random House, 1986.

Henry David Thoreau. *Walden and Other Writings*. New York: Barnes & Noble Books, 1993.

Eckhart Tolle. *The Power of Now: A Guide to Spiritual Enlightenment*. Novato, CA.: New World Library, 1999.

Anne Truitt. *Daybook: The Journal of an Artist*. New York: Random House, 1982.

Kurt Vonnegut. *A Man Without a Country*. New York: Seven Stories Press, 2005.

Gary Zukav *The Seat of the Soul*. New York: Simon & Schuster, 1990.

Postscript

At the beginning of my writing career, I used to prowl around bookstores, examining the back flap copy on book jackets, where an author's brief biography and photograph are displayed. Maybe it was simply the fashion of the day to describe all those Vermont farmsteads and golden retrievers playing around the edges of these writers' lives, and perhaps not all of them had a tenured teaching job at a major college or university, but virtually all the men and nearly all the women writers I admired had one asset in common—a devoted partner who could support them (presumably with cash money), should the writer's wits get frayed. It was a bit depressing.

Newly divorced, with children to support and the economic know-how of a frog (I used to mistakenly think that the high interest on credit cards accrued to me), I feared for my own emotional and economic survival. But after a while I realized the obvious, that it was counterproductive and ungrateful to count other writers' blessings, particularly when I had so many of my own.

Now my life contains a partner. He was a long time arriving, but worth the wait. During our courtship, most of my creativity went into trying to decide whether we were meant to be together, but once we arranged our coffee cups under the same roof, my writing life reemerged. This book is the first fruit of that new life.